THE
LAST LIGHT
BREAKING

THE
LAST LIGHT
BREAKING

▲▲▲▲▲▲▲▲▲

Living Among Alaska's
Inupiat Eskimos

NICK JANS

ALASKA NORTHWEST BOOKS™
Anchorage • Seattle • Portland

Library of Congress Cataloging-in-Publication Data

Second printing 1994

Jans, Nick, 1955–
    The last light breaking : living among Alaska's Inupiat Eskimos /
Nick Jans
        p. cm.
    Includes bibliographical references.
    ISBN 0-88240-445-8
    ISBN 0-88240-458-X (paper)
    1. Kobuk River Region (Alaska)—Description and travel.
    2. Eskimos—Alaska—Kobuk River Region. I. Title.
F912.K6J36 1993
979.8'6—dc20   93–8041
                                                              CIP

Edited by Ellen Harkins Wheat
Cover and book design by Bergh Jensen
Map by Vikki Lieb

Jacket photos: Front cover: *Caribou in the Brooks Range.* Photograph by Michio
Hoshino, courtesy of Minden Pictures. Back flap: *Author Nick Jans with arctic char,
on the Hunt River in the Brooks Range.* Photograph by Steve Pilz.

ALASKA NORTHWEST BOOKS™
An imprint of Graphic Arts Center Publishing Company
Editorial office: 2208 NW Market Street, Suite 300, Seattle, WA 98107
Catalog and order dept.: P.O. Box 10306, Portland, OR 97210
    800-452-3032

Printed on recycled paper in the United States of America

To the elders, who remember

CONTENTS

⌃⌃⌃⌃⌃⌃⌃⌃⌃

PREFACE

As soon as I saw this country, I knew I had to write about it. I remember sitting outside my tent at Walker Lake in 1979, swatting mosquitoes and waiting for the arctic muses to whisper something profound. Uncertain of where to begin or what to say, I stuck to the obvious—the fish we'd caught, how strange it was to see the sun at midnight, how "massive, stunning, and utterly wild" the mountains were, how my friend Peter and I were off on "the adventure of a lifetime." I'm not sure I bought what I wrote even then, but I knew I had to come up with something.

Over the next five years I hammered out a pile of notebooks filled with purplish prose. After the first (and richly deserved) rejection, I kept my writing to myself, painfully aware that I had nothing original to say about this harsh, magical land; in fact, I was becoming less and less sure of what I felt or believed about anything. Still I watched and listened and jotted stuff down, figuring that someday a switch would click and it all would make sense.

Of course, I was missing the point. In a place where distant peaks sometimes appear inverted above the horizon, where you could walk for hours toward a hill you'd guessed was a mile away, where the sun rises at all points of the compass and sometimes casts pale ghosts of itself, nothing would or *could* ever be certain; in this world the laws of physics seemed to float freely, compressing and expanding, refusing logic. At first these ambiguities gnawed at me, but slowly I learned to let go. The Inupiat had always moved within these eddying currents of time, space, and light; to them, insubstantiality wasn't a question, but a fact of life. Anthropologist Edwin S. Hall writes:

In a land where summer fogs blur the distinction between land and sea, where winter wind and snow can produce the condition known as "white-out"—when the land and sky cannot be separated . . . the concept of an ever-changing, amorphous world is not surprising. The Eskimo world was essentially smooth, without projections or sharp corners. Apparent transformations of various kinds were always occurring, so the change of a man to a wolf was no more unbelievable or inexplicable than the merging of land and sea. If an Eskimo were tricked by lighting conditions into thinking a ground squirrel was a grizzly bear and suddenly discovered he was looking at the smaller animal, the most obvious explanation was that a bear transformed itself, probably through magic, into a ground squirrel.

Having stalked a few squirrel-bears myself, in arranging this collection of essays from different years I've decided to abandon linear organization in favor of circular rhythms, more thematic than chronological. These writings, like traditional Inupiat narrative, have a tendency to circle back, as the land itself does, through the coming and going of geese, whitefish, and caribou.

I've anglicized the spellings of some Inupiaq words for the sake of simplicity. The epigraphs are gleaned from many sources; some are purely biographical, others are snatches of folktales, and a few drift in the spaces between.

In "Ambler Trading" and "Arctic Heroes," I've changed several names to protect identities; otherwise, this book is a work of nonfiction. For every story here, a dozen remain untold, and I still have more questions than answers.

ACKNOWLEDGMENTS

I owe thanks to many people: first and foremost to Jennifer Maier, whose unfailing friendship, literary judgment, and patience over the phone carried me through first drafts and lonely nights; to Lynn and Carol Norstadt, whose door was always open, and whose advice was always good; to John McDermott and Bert Shuster, who listened to me rave; to David Bosworth and Jack Brenner, who taught me something; to Giselle Smith, Grant Sims, and Tobin Morrison, who gave me a chance; to Marlene Blessing and Ellen Wheat, who believed in me; and to Steve Pilz, Mark Pope, and the rest of the Ambler School staff, who put up with me.

To the people of Ambler and Noatak go my deepest thanks, especially to Clarence Wood, who showed me more than I can remember and answered too many questions; to Minnie Gray and Sarah Tickett, who shared their joy in simple things; to Nelson and Edna Griest, who made me feel I belonged. There are many more, both Inupiat and *naluaqmiut*, I want to thank for being good neighbors and friends over the past fourteen years; I would mention names, but the list would go on for more pages than I'm allowed. When I think of you all, I realize how blessed I have been to live among you. *Taiku.*

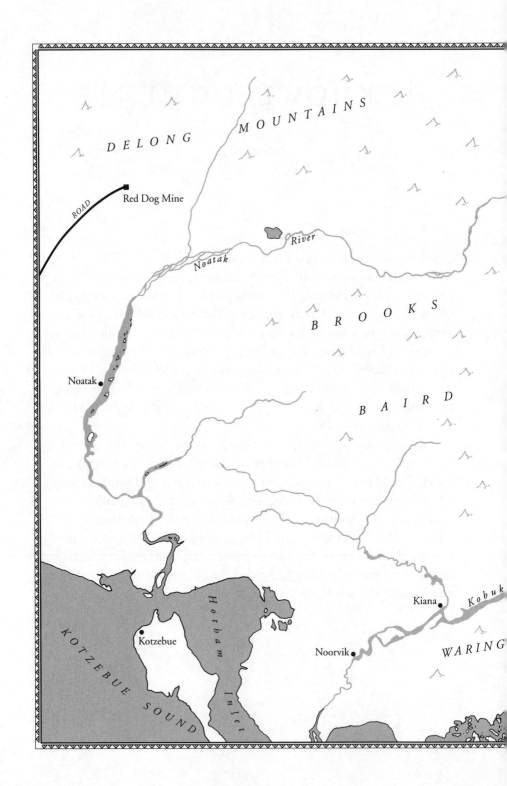

THE AMBLER REGION

THE
LAST LIGHT
BREAKING

I will walk with leg muscles
which are strong
as the sinews of the shins of the little caribou calf.
I will walk with leg muscles
which are strong
as the sinews of the shins of the little hare.
I will take care not to go towards the dark.
I will go towards the day.

—Iglulik Eskimo words to be spoken
when setting out on a long journey,
The Report of the Fifth Thule Expedition
1921-1924

Getting Here

▵▵▵▵▵▵▵▵▵

Alaska?" says the gray-haired woman. "How exciting!" She puts her book aside, ready to talk.

Thirty thousand feet below, Illinois slides past. I lean back and sigh; there's no place to hide, and she reminds me of my favorite aunt. There's nothing to do but answer her questions and pretend I haven't heard them before. As a matter of fact, I've had the same conversation three times in the past two days. It's part of the ritual when you travel Outside.

"Where in Alaska?"

"Ambler. A little Eskimo village in the upper left-hand corner."

Here it comes.

"How fascinating! Do Eskimos really live in igloos?"

Bingo. "Well, *iglu* is the Inupiaq word for house. Alaskan Eskimos never did live in ice houses, like you see in the movies." *Now, about the cold.*

"How cold is it up there?"

"Thirty to seventy below in January."

"How do you start your car?"

"There aren't any cars. The nearest highway is about three hundred miles away."

"Goodness! How many years have you been there?"

"Going on thirteen."

There's nothing wrong with her questions; thirteen years ago I might have asked the same ones. Explaining over and over, though, drains my patience. I give my usual answers, and get irritated with the sound of my own voice. But I smile and go on.

When the questions get into details, the nitty-gritty of everyday in the arctic, life seems like a long list of "no's"—no running water or flush toilets, no shopping malls, restaurants, bars, movie theaters—none of the things people take for granted. Finally, the woman looks at me oddly and shakes her head. "How on earth did you end up there?"

"I don't know."

The truth is, I really *don't* know. It's a question I ask myself from time to time, but I've learned not to expect a good answer.

At least I know how it started. In 1979, two years out of college, not sure what should come next, I packed up my '66 Plymouth, threw my canoe on the roof, and rattled north, drawn by the stock images of Alaska we all carry with us—polar bears and wolves, Eskimos and kayaks, endless mountains, rivers full of fish. But I'd bought maps and done some reading, too; I aimed for the western Brooks Range because there was hardly anybody there, and because there was something magical about the names on the map—Igikpak, Natmaktugiaq, Ipnelivik, Nuna—Eskimo words I didn't even know how to pronounce. I figured I could drive as far as Fairbanks, where I planned to meet a friend from college days. We'd hire a bush plane to drop us off at the headwaters of the Kobuk River, and take it from there.

I had no idea I'd stay. All these years later, in the middle of splitting wood, or walking to school, or stalking a band of caribou, I'll suddenly realize where I am, and shake my head. It was going to be just a year. I had a girl back in Maine, vague plans for law school and the sort of life I'd been raised to live. But when that first year was up, I decided on one more, and another after that. I wasn't procrastinating. I just knew I wasn't ready to leave. Friends came and went; my girl back east got married; my parents got exasperated. Next year, I told them.

What I didn't tell them, because I didn't know it, was that I'd fallen in love. I wasn't going anywhere because this was where I was supposed to be. It took me five years to figure that out.

When I first saw the upper Kobuk country, I have to admit I was a little disappointed. The Brooks Range just to the north was postcard wilderness, but the valley where I was going to live was wet tundra, scraggly forest, and low, unspectacular hills. Where were all the bears and caribou? You could cast into a perfect fishing hole for an hour without a nudge, find oil drums and surveyors' benchmarks in the middle of nowhere. Ambler was a jumble of cabins and prefab houses, each ringed by piles of junk machinery, trash, and the ubiquitous oil drums. Upstream and down were other villages, more or less the same.

As the months drifted by, though, I realized I hadn't been paying attention. The arctic flowed in subtle rhythms, and I slowly learned to relax, to listen, and to move with it. A barren stretch of tundra might, in another season, ripple with thousands of migrating caribou, or shimmer with blueberries. A pool in a river, empty one month, boiled with salmon the next. I learned to study a hillside until I knew each bush and shadow. Then I saw the bears and moose, moving quietly about their business. And everywhere there was clarity, an exquisite purity of light. Cast in its glow, the landscape became surreal, dreamlike, timeless.

Even the village had its own functional beauty. Life here was unaffected and direct. What I'd mistaken for sloppiness was utility; today's oil drum was tomorrow's dog pot or stove, and a rusty bedframe was angle iron for a sled hitch. I learned, too, that cars and flush toilets were geegaws instead of necessities, and that a steady procession of chores—chopping wood, hauling water, tinkering with chain saws—was comforting. You seldom had to wonder *why;* the facts of living were self-evident.

As a storekeeper, then as a schoolteacher and basketball coach in both Noatak and Ambler, I slowly became part of Eskimo village life. I taught the Inupiat children as they taught me; I learned the musical patois called village English, and how to say "yes" by raising my eyebrows. The parents and grandparents laughed at my comical first efforts with snowmobiles and rifles, then showed me what they knew. Once they found I wasn't another teacher staying a year and passing through, they would ask, whenever I'd leave, "When are you coming home?"

Still, after all these years, there is the loneliness, the silence that both fills and empties the spirit, the desolation of fifty below zero, the knowledge that no matter how long I stay I'll always be an outsider. Alone in my cabin on a winter night, I wonder if I've missed out somehow. Then I remember the Jade Mountains glowing at twilight, and know that this is my home, the only place I could ever be.

Nowadays young folks cannot go anywhere if they are out of gasoline. Here along the Kobuk the kayak was an important means of transportation. As long as you had a kayak, it would take you anywhere. Sometimes it even seemed like a motorboat because it was so easy to maneuver. . . . We had no problem traveling by kayak in those days. Nowadays it's not the same.

Fishing and trapping were the only means of subsistence in those days. People would go up beyond Noatak to hunt for caribou because there were none around here. Now no one goes beyond Noatak to hunt.

. . . During the winter the men went trapping. For transportation they used dog teams rather than snow machines. Snowshoes were also essential for getting around on the snow.

. . . Nowadays, young men might find it hard to hunt this way. Everything is easy to get. Today you can just reach out and get it off a shelf.

—from the narrative of
Lawrence Akisaqpak Gray,
in *Lore of the Inupiat*

Ambler Trading

▲▲▲▲▲▲▲▲▲

As the Munz Islander clattered down the gravel, I pressed my nose to the glass for a glimpse of the Ambler airport: a windsock and a few Eskimos waiting by a pickup truck—the only one in town, I'd soon learn. Behind them was a metal equipment shed, a pile of fuel drums, and a lone Cessna, ringed by an enormous sweep of trees, mountains, and sky. The plane ground to a halt, the squeal of brakes rousing the drunk who'd been snoring behind me. I'd spent most of the past hour suffering through his boozy proclamations, shouted into my ear over the engines' racket. Somehow, he looked familiar. Later on, I'd recognize him in both his official and unofficial capacities—Enoch Harding, constable of Ambler and eminent bootlegger. I followed Enoch's weaving progress out through the clutter of mailbags and boxes that filled half the fuselage. Except for the pilot I was the only white face, but everyone seemed friendly as I stepped into the bright August sun.

"Are you the new teacher?" A big man smiled, holding out his hand.

"No. The new store manager," I replied, smiling back and holding out mine.

"Ambler Trading?" His mouth tightened, and the big man turned his back.

Suddenly no one else was smiling either, and I was left wondering where to put my hand. Someone muttered in Inupiaq, and the staggering constable declared, "Ah, he's all right. He's a gooood guy." I stuffed the empty hand into a pocket and pretended to watch the pilot unloading freight. Actually, I was eyeing the distance between me and the plane door. But my pack was already in the truck, and I was broke anyway, five thousand miles from home. I scrambled over the pickup's tailgate.

"Five bucks, white man." The big man held out his hand again, this time palm up. "If you work for that German, you pay."

I could tell it was no use explaining that Erik was Dutch. As I trudged down the hill with my pack, eating the pickup's dust, I had the feeling that I'd just started to pay.

Thirteen years later, thumbing through my journals, I wonder what kept me from jumping back on that plane. Twenty-four years old, barely three months in Alaska, I was as alone as I've ever been— 50 miles above the arctic circle, 200 miles from the nearest road, and it had taken me less than a minute in town to get the bum's rush. I had no way of knowing that this place would become my home, or that someday people would call "Welcome back!" and cross the road to shake my hand. I had no way of knowing that the mountains would get inside me, that one day I'd navigate by their shapes and see them in my sleep. Still, I must have known something to get here the way I did—pounding across Canada and up the Alaska Highway in a '66 Plymouth, abandoning it in Fairbanks, then pitching in my last two hundred bucks with my friend Peter Torres for a floatplane charter to the Kobuk's headwaters. Now the canoe trip, 700-odd miles, was over and Peter was gone, headed back east.

Of course, I had a job. Erik VanVeenen, arctic entrepreneur and big game guide, had hired me to manage the mercantile branch of his empire—the cluttered frame building, barely more than a shack, called Ambler Trading. And it was a rented shack at that. Actually, it was the Ambler Community Building, and the city council's plan had been to let Erik use it for a month or two, until his own store was completed. That should have happened by now, but this was, after all, the arctic, and Erik's grand construction plan was running a bit late. Say, six months late. The city council was getting restless. Most of them hadn't liked the idea in the first place, and the building known simply as The Community was, as its name suggested, a center for civic activities—city council meetings, for example.

And, as I was to learn, there was a faction in the village that didn't want any *naluaqmiut*—white people—here at all. A local holy man named Maniilaq had predicted, before the turn of the century, that a great city would rise at this exact place. Pale strangers who rode through the sky in chairs would flock here in great numbers, following the discovery of something valuable in the earth. There had already been a sudden (if modest) influx of white homesteaders over the last three decades, enough to raise concern. But these *naluaqmiut,* roughly two dozen, seemed hardly a threat. Scattered up and downriver, most had adopted the traditional lifestyle—living in sod houses, mushing dogs, and living off the land—even as their Inupiat neighbors adopted snowmobiles, frame houses, and store food. But now came Erik VanVeenen, charming, ruthless, and ambitious, planning to erect a two-story white man's monument in the center of town. An increasing number of *Ivisaappaatmiut* (Ambler People) saw Erik as the embodiment of Maniilaq's prophecy, if not the devil incarnate.

To make matters worse, Erik was a big game guide, competing, people said, for the animals on which they'd always depended. His hunters, mostly German and Swiss, walked around town, jabbering in unknown tongues. At the first city council meeting I attended, an unsuccessful motion was raised to boot Erik out of town. At the second, there was a motion requesting that all white people leave. The second was directly related to the first, just as I, by dint of association, was directly related to Erik—a brother or cousin, perhaps.

The store was the same as I'd remembered from my brief visit in July—an anarchy of peanut butter and sleeping bags, fishing rods, chamber pots and dog chains; guns and stereos and dolls and rubber boots, coffee and cereal and canned milk piled to the low ceiling on rickety metal shelves. Cases of fruit, dish soap, and soda pop teetered in the narrow aisles. From the inside, I had the impression that the outside walls were bulging, the way they would in a cartoon.

Behind the metal counter by the door sat Erik, the unshaven monarch of all he surveyed. Brushing the crumbs from his moustache, he rose to greet me with a boyish grin, holding out an open box of glazed doughnuts. "How vas the trip? Good, good. Vell, I have hunters coming next week, and I need to pound some nails over at the new store. My dad and nephew are over from Holland, helping out. Just throw your stuff in the back. Here's a list of prices, and I'll show you how to use the register. Don't let any kids out of your sight—the little buggers will steal us blind. If you have any time between customers, get some stock up on the shelves wherever it'll fit. All set? Good. It vill all get done. I'll check up on you later." As he hurried out the door and up the street, anxious and bearlike, I could practically see the gears turning in his head.

I propped my pack in the corner that would be home for the next four months. There was a Coleman camp stove and a few dishes on a shelf, a couple of folding chairs, and a rolled up sleeping pad. One covered bucket held water, and the other one in the closet was the nearest I'd get to a flush toilet. The loaded shelves loomed overhead, casting shadows off bare bulbs in the ceiling. It would be like camping in a warehouse. On the other hand, with all this stuff around, I wasn't likely to starve.

I wandered down the four tiny aisles, taking stock and checking prices as I waited for my first customer. A six-pack of Coke was six dollars, a dozen eggs, two fifty. A three-pound box of Banquet frozen fried chicken (one of the big sellers, Erik told me) cost nine dollars; a half gallon of ice cream, six bucks. This was 1979. Was I really going to sell a can of beans for one ninety? Down the hill at Cleveland Trading, our only competition, prices were noticeably lower, but the shelves were half bare. Later, when I asked Erik how he set his prices, he showed me how he used a calculator to add 33 percent to wholesale, plus air freight—300 miles' worth. Then he tacked on a bit more, anywhere from 5 to 20 percent.

"What's that?" I asked.

"Bullshit tax," Erik said, with a wink. "A little extra for putting up with the bullshit." The exact amount of bullshit tax depended on the day.

A patter of footsteps announced my first customer—a skinny little girl, maybe four years old, with long black hair and a runny nose. She regarded the strange *naluaqmiu* before her with alarm. When I smiled, she steadied herself and solemnly laid a grubby handful of change on the counter, still eyeing me warily. In my best storekeeper's voice, I asked her what she needed today.

Silence.

"Candy?" I prompted.

She didn't answer, but her eyes widened at the array behind the counter—cases of Milky Ways, Twizzlers, Drax Snax, LifeSavers, Garbage Can-dy—at least twenty varieties.

"Which one?"

More wide-eyed silence.

"This one?"

The child seemed to be on the verge of glaucoma.

"What about this one?"

Finally in exasperation I laid a Drax Snax and some Twizzlers on the counter and sorted out her change. With an expression of complete ecstasy the pretty little girl opened her mouth, exposing a row of blackened stumps. I'd just met my first candy junkie.

It took me a couple weeks to figure out that she'd been talking to me all along. The Inupiat are subtle, quiet people, and much of their communication hinges on nonverbal cues. Raising the eyebrows or widening the eyes means yes; a wrinkled nose is a negative. The poor girl had been shouting at me, "Yes! Yes! YES!" All these years later, I still recall that first simple failure to understand; it reminds me of all my failures since then, and of the distance that remains.

A steady trickle of customers came and went, mostly kids wanting candy and pop, or young men buying cigarettes. Total sales, I figured, had to be less than a hundred dollars for the day, and the 6:00 P.M. closing time was less than two hours off. I began to wonder why Erik was bothering to build a bigger store when this one seemed scarcely worth the trouble.

Then, as if someone had opened a spigot, the store was flooded with people, adults and teenagers and kids and old women, many of them piling small fortunes in cans and boxes on the counter. "Checks come!" someone said. One after another, people bought a hundred dollars' worth of groceries—enough to fill a large cardboard carton or two—and pushed crisp computer-printed checks toward me. This batch, which had apparently arrived on the same plane I had, was issued by the state: blue unemployment checks and green longevity bonus awards. On other days it would be federal welfare checks, or NANA Corporation dividends, or Alaska Permanent Fund shares, or food stamps. Although at least 80 percent of the village was unemployed, thousands of dollars flooded into the village in biweekly gouts. Here was a cash economy without cash, virtually without jobs, fueled by some vast, invisible machine to the south.

I rang up totals, filled boxes, and made change; in the absence of a bank, a new currency had been invented, one based on recycled checks—some tattered with handling—and small amounts of equally worn dollars. Some checks bore dates a month old; some dollar bills were the texture of felt, dog-eared and patched with tape. Yet they were accepted, as were the IOUs I wrote when the change ran thin.

Calling this place a trading post was only slightly romantic; Erik also accepted furs, birchbark baskets, and loads of firewood—their value measured against the store's retail prices, of course, and payable only in merchandise or credit. Only two generations separated him from men like Walter Blankenship and Warren Ferguson, pioneer traders in the region who'd exchanged bolts of calico, steel axes, and sacks of flour for beaver pelts.

Just before closing time, with a dozen people still in the store, two drunks wandered in. Though Ambler was a dry town, all sales of alcohol illegal, the flow of bootleg booze was as steady as the checks. There was no law against importation, and Enoch the constable wasn't about to arrest himself or anyone else for doing a little trading of their own. A pint of Bacardi 151-proof rum might go for a hundred bucks, or double that late at night. Just now, it seemed, rum couldn't be had at any price. The two drunks, both young men, shakily gathered my entire stock of mouthwash, cough syrup, and vanilla extract—all alcohol based—and stacked the bottles on the counter. One old woman stopped fanning herself with a ptarmigan wing long enough to scold them soundly in Inupiaq. Bleary-eyed, swaying, they waited for her to finish and for me to ring up a sale.

"C'mon, *naluaqmiu,* let's go," one slurred. I shook my head and started gathering up the bottles.

"Hey, we gonna buy that!"

"No, you're not. Go home."

"We'll kick your ass, you white shit!"

It had already been a long first day, and I wasn't interested in capping it off with a brawl. The drunks, sensing my indecision, redoubled their threats, and one balled his fists. Suddenly a shrill voice cried out. It was the old woman with the ptarmigan wing fan. Stooped and squinting, she launched into a tirade that needed no translation. Another customer, a handsome middle-aged woman, joined her. "You boys go home!" she said in English. Off balance, the drunks staggered out, muttering.

"*Adii,*" said the old woman. "They shouldn't do that." Her name, she told me, was Maude Foxglove. When I held out my hand, she took it.

Two days later, just before opening time, I was busy with sweeping and straightening when someone thumped on the door. At first I ignored the racket, figuring it was an impatient kid who could wait another fifteen minutes for his candy fix. But the pounding didn't stop. When I finally slid the bolt, a young Eskimo man burst in, wearing only a pair of jeans and an expression of sheer panic. "Someone sure bullshit me!" he muttered, panting.

"Hey, what's . . . "

"Man, he's coming!"

"Who?"

"Mike Junior. I just wake up and he's pointing shotgun at me. Someone say I was fooling around with Susie. Quick, he's coming!"

"Hey, that's not my job. Where's the cop?"

He shrugged nervously. "Drunk, I guess."

"Okay, get in the back." As I bolted the door and loaded a shotgun off the rack, I felt like I was acting out a cheap western. I crouched by the window, peering out at a short guy with glasses and a gun that seemed as long as he was tall. His expression was grim and purposeful as he poked around the bushes outside the store and finally, to my great relief, stalked off. Half an hour later my half-naked guest decided the coast was clear, and I opened for business as usual.

Over the next six months I'd be an unwilling participant in four more "Gunsmoke" scenarios. Although the *Ivisaappaatmiut* are gentle people, firearms seem a natural form of expression. People shoot outside their houses on New Year's Eve, or down at the river when the ice goes out; kids handle rifles the way white kids handle baseball bats, and grow up surrounded by the carcasses of caribou, moose, and bear. A successful hunter is, and always has been, a success in a larger sense: he provides, in both symbol and substance, the means by which The People survive. So it's not surprising that a drunk young man sometimes reaches for what he remembers as best.

I confess that I wasn't mulling over the psychology of drunken gunplay that morning, or any of the other times I found myself clutching Erik's Drielling—a triple-barreled monster that could flatten a grizzly—as howls and gunshots echoed in the night. The nearest cavalry were the state troopers in Kotzebue. If the satellite phone were working, if the weather were flyable, and if they weren't already called out, Dan Weatherly and Kim Nay would grab their flak vests, jump in a Cessna, and be here in an hour or two. By that time, the ruckus had usually blown over; it was almost always a lone drunk spraying bullets at the sky, and once he was out of shells, things would calm down.

By some miracle, no one got shot that winter, though there were some close calls—a staggering teenager emptying a lever-action carbine into a house full of people, one bullet just missing a toddler; a drunk I'd thrown out earlier battering the store door with a shotgun butt, screaming my name and blasting off shells as I lay on the floor, knuckles white around the Drielling. Before the troopers hauled him off around dawn, he took a roomful of friends hostage and stabbed two people with a screwdriver.

One evening I added my two cents to the general mayhem. I was sitting alone, cleaning rifles after a hunt, running patches down bores and wiping away smudges. I'd checked them all first, of course, and emptied each magazine. Maybe I was tired, or maybe it was the Jack Daniels I was nipping, but when I picked up Erik's .30-06 Sauer carbine, worked the action, and casually squeezed the trigger, it erupted in my hands. Somehow I'd missed the last bullet.

I sat openmouthed, staring at the dark hole I'd punched in the closet door. Behind that door was the town's phone relay, twenty thousand dollars' worth of electronics. The bullet—a 200-grain Nosler—had missed it by an inch, plowed on through the wall into the adjacent clinic, two feet over the heads of a visiting doctor and his wife as they lay in bed, and disappeared out the far wall. They accepted my stumbling apology, but there was nothing I could say to the small crowd of grim-faced villagers who'd come running. I'd just joined the Accidental Discharge Club, and they didn't let me forget it for months. Not only was I Erik's cousin, but an idiot and a menace to society.

In the bright summer evenings after work I strolled around town, watching, learning, and listening, trying to match names and faces. It took a while, since few people ever bothered to introduce themselves. They didn't mean to be rude; everyone here had known everyone else all their lives. Naturally they assumed I'd know their names. No one bothered to identify themselves over the phone or CB radio either. You were supposed to recognize the voice.

The village was perched on a high bank just below the confluence of the Ambler and Kobuk rivers—perhaps three dozen buildings scattered among clumps of birch and spruce, connected by a grid of rough gravel lanes and winding footpaths. About a third of the houses were new prefabricated models funded by oil revenues and federal subsidies. Most families who'd signed up had gotten a house. The log cabins and sod *ivruliks* that had once been home were now storage caches piled with bundles of dried fish and caribou, junk snowmobile parts, and fuel drums. A few people had built their own frame houses—some of these little more than plywood shacks—and others had kept their cabins. The largest building by far was the new high school, scheduled to open in September; students who'd been sent off to boarding schools could take classes at home for the first time. Across the road Erik's new store was taking shape, and the airstrip I'd landed on was just two years old, and then there was the white satellite dish that brought in a single channel of television four hours a day. All around the village there was that sense of newness and change. New buildings seemed to be sprouting up, even as the *ivruliks* they'd replaced were sinking back into the land. Beyond, mountains and tundra rolled off to the horizon, endless as the sky.

Ambler, I learned, was new itself—founded in 1958, by far the youngest of eleven villages in the region, and one of the youngest in the state. Following a bitter political feud, six families from Shungnak had banded together to start their own village. The site they chose, twenty-five miles to the west, was a rich one—good places for gillnets, plenty of firewood, and fine hunting; twice a year, the tundra around town was awash in waves of migrating caribou. And so the new village of *Ivisaappaat,* officially known as Ambler, had grown and prospered, a community of proud, independent people—independent, at times, to the point of anarchy.

I'd been in Ambler less than two weeks when the cash bag disappeared. One evening after a walk I reached under the counter—there was no safe—and the blue cloth bag holding four days' receipts, over $2,500 in food stamps, cash, and checks, was gone. A panicky search turned up nothing. The back door hung ajar. I sprinted up the road to tell Erik, my life as a storekeeper passing before my eyes. He was livid, but it was a clear case of burglary, and, with a full load of hunting clients coming in, he needed me. The next day a teenage boy turned in a handful of checks he said he'd found in the bushes, and when the troopers grilled him, he caved in. It wasn't his first break-in; he and a friend had knocked off the post office, too. The troopers hauled them away in cuffs.

Village elders shook their heads. Stealing like this, one told me, hadn't existed a generation ago. Nobody locked their houses; they propped an ax or broom against the door to show they weren't home, and no one would think of entering. But now there were more temptations. Inevitably the thieves were young men, looking for cash, gasoline, booze, or things that could be sold without a trace—wolf skins, for example. Most of them wanted money for marijuana, which sold for ten to fifteen dollars a joint. Almost all the crime in the region, the troopers said, was tied to drugs or alcohol.

As the weeks went by, I slipped into the rhythms of storekeeping and village life—quiet mornings stocking shelves and sweeping, bursts of frenetic activity when food stamps or checks came, relaxed conversations with customers during slow stretches. Few people seemed to be in a hurry; time here was too large to be chopped, like kindling, into minutes and hours. And, except for a dozen school and city jobs—all funded by outside money—there were no clocks to punch, nothing to rush off to. Folks ate when they were hungry, slept when they were tired, and subsisted on resources as they became available: fish, geese, caribou, unemployment checks, and food stamps, all in season. If there was no check, there was always the land. The *Ivisaappaatmiut* responded to the twentieth century just as they had to the sixteenth: in times of plenty, they were extravagant; in lean times, they hunkered. Slowly, inevitably, as if by osmosis, my pulse rate slowed to match my surroundings.

In a bush village, everyone ends up at the store sooner or later— old women, kids, pilots, drunks, teachers, and itinerant dentists. If there's a new face in town, or if someone's had a baby or been arrested, you can wait behind the counter and the news will come to you. There's a strange bond between storekeeper and customer; as I boxed groceries or made change, people told me their troubles, often in such shocking detail that I felt like a priest hearing confession. Even when I didn't want to listen, there wasn't much choice. I was a captive audience. I knew more than I wanted about everyone's finances, too; who was getting regular paychecks, who was on hard times, and who had just won a poker game. Sooner or later, all the money in town passed through my hands. I broke checks, extended credit, and, in emergencies, made loans. Erik seldom charged interest, and didn't have to. Interest was included in the bullshit tax.

The brief autumn burned bright and faded into brown; in early October the first snow came, and ice floes whispered down the Kobuk. Erik was seldom around, and I was on my own for weeks at a time. I sat behind the counter, played basketball in the school gym, hunted caribou, and made short forays into the country by boat and snowmobile. By November I knew the names of everyone in town, and by December I was sick of being a storekeeper. Ahead lay the dark loneliness of my first arctic winter. One afternoon as the snow whirled in deepening drifts around the steps of Ambler Trading, I listened to the stove hiss, stared at the dusty clutter of shelves, and made plans to jump on the next plane out. I had no idea what the hell I was doing here, or why I should stay. I could be in Seattle in two days, and back east in three.

The door creaked open, and in teetered old Maude Foxglove in her bright calico parka. Breathing heavily, she plunked down in a chair and drew out her ptarmigan wing fan. "I come to get some few small stuffs," she said. "*Aarigaa* (good) to see you." As she sat by the stove, fanning herself and sweating, I gathered her groceries for her and stacked them on the counter. Outside, the wind shuddered against the store. I rang up the total, packed everything in a box, and waited for Maude to hand me her state longevity bonus check. As I made change, she told me about making mukluks, and then we sat, listening to the storm, waiting for her grandson to come and pick up her box. She was in no hurry, and by the time she left, neither was I.

The old people also said that the salmon don't actually die. I don't know how they knew this, but this knowledge must have been passed down for many generations by word of mouth. They said that salmon don't actually die. Instead, it is said that the inner being of the salmon leaves its old boat, or physical body, and enters the body of a land animal. They then travel overland to the north until they reach the ocean, where they depart from the shore, once again in the form of salmon. This is what the people said about them long ago.

. . . There are many other things that were handed down by word of mouth that I can still relate but often forget each time I speak into the tape recorder. Also, I am doing this at a time when I do forget easily. That is how life is and I'm trying to tell as much as I can. I have told what I have heard about the life of fish which was known from a long time ago. That is all I will say for now about fish.

—Robert Nasruk Cleveland and
Donald Foote, *Stories of the Black
River People*

Black River Autumn

▲▲▲▲▲▲▲▲▲

T he September day is fading as I round the bend below Minnie Gray's fish camp, halfway between the Alaskan arctic villages of Ambler and Shungnak. Chilled after a thirty-mile run up the Kobuk, I'm happy to see the familiar high bank and ramshackle cache that marks the mouth of Black River. My friends Minnie and Sarah, two Inupiat women from Ambler, are expecting me. They plan to spend the next two days subsistence fishing with seine and gillnet, as they have each fall for the past fifty years. I'm here to help with the heavy lifting and pulling, and, on Minnie's insistence, I've brought my rifle.

"*Achaqan,* those bears," she says. "One might come around."

As I pull into the mouth of Black River, a small slough that drains a stretch of tundra on the south side of the Kobuk, the women are already at work, checking the two gillnets they've set. The floats twitch and bob with struggling fish. Minnie straightens up and smiles, her handsome features glowing in the low sun.

"Look, we get big *siilik!*" she calls, holding up a fat, ten-pound pike.

"*Aarigaa,* lots of fish!" says Sarah.

I anchor and watch them work down the net, two moving as one as they pull a section over the gunwale of their aluminum boat, untangle fish, and toss them into washtubs, gloved hands nimble despite the cold. Small pike and humpback whitefish make up most of the catch, with a few arctic grayling and *kalusraak* (least cisco) mixed in. Then something big thrashes in the net. Sarah reaches for her stick and clubs a sheefish as long as her leg.

"We hardly get that kind in here," she says, hoisting it aboard by the gills.

In twenty minutes the women have picked nearly two washtubs of fish, then worked back down, straightening and resetting. Each fifty-foot net is weighted by standard leadline and short sections of caribou antler. A century ago, it would have been handwoven from willow bark and floated with wood. Now, life is easier—aluminum skiffs instead of skin or birchbark boats, outboards for harnessed dogs and pushpoles.

Fish have always been important to the upper Kobuk Eskimos. Waterfowl, caribou, and moose have their place, but fish—dried in strips, boiled in chunks, baked ungutted, fermented, or frozen and eaten raw, sliced thin with seal oil—is a staple in any season. Gathering them is the traditional work of women, while hunting is left to the men.

After Minnie and Sarah are done checking net, we take care of chores—sawing firewood, hauling water, unpacking gear. Camp is a rickety log cache and, further back, a wooden frame covered by the weathered remains of a canvas wall tent, overlaid with plastic tarps. At the edge of the high bank, where the river has gnawed in, is the ruin of another cache, poles splayed into the air.

"I was raised here," says Minnie, looking out across the river. Her father, Robert Cleveland, moved here from Shungnak in the 1930s, when she was a young girl. I can see why he picked this place. The camp commands a huge sweep of water, land, and sky, framed by the peaks along the Brooks Range's southern flank. The mouth of the Black is a fine spot for a gillnet, and the slough itself is a funnel for game—caribou, moose, bear—and migrating waterfowl.

Just now, the light is magical, slanting in golden from the south. In the past week, the land's breathing has slowed; everything is settling, turning inward. Even the wind seems to have drifted off to sleep. The Kobuk flows past, cold and clear in the dusk.

"No more geese flying," Minnie says. "Ice will come soon."

Inside the tent, we eat dried whitefish and canned ham by the light of a kerosene lantern. The woodstove, made from a cut-off oil drum, crackles and pops, and the CB radio in the corner answers. The women listen to static-filled conversations, occasionally laughing or joining in when they hear a familiar voice. People listening along the upper Kobuk know that Minnie and Sarah are in camp, as they have been every fall for as long as anyone remembers. It's a small marker in the rhythm of the seasons, a comforting reminder that some things never change. The conversations go on for a time; finally, Sarah picks up the microphone. "Good night from Black River," she says, and replying goodnights trail in before she clicks off the switch.

We unroll foam mattresses and bedding on the plywood floor, and I crawl into my sleeping bag. "Story time," Minnie says, and we lie in the dark, trading tales. Once she was staying here alone and heard wolves on the tundra, the howls growing louder and closer in the darkness. She brought her dog inside, quieted it, and built a fire in the stove. The wind carried the smoke to the wolf pack, and they left. Another time, she was checking net when a rutting bull moose charged from the willows. She dropped it at forty yards with her .30-30.

As I listen to stories of dogsled journeys, storms, hauls of fish, and people long dead, I can hear in the voices of these two aging widows a longing for life that has passed by, and for the old ways that will be lost with their generation. Few Inupiat under forty know how to handle a seine, and no one is learning; children and grandchildren are more interested in television, dances, and basketball at the village gym, or they've moved away. Many have turned to alcohol and drugs. Only a few dozen elders remember the solitude of winter camp, or the aroma of black bear intestines roasting on a stick. "I don't know what's wrong with all the kids," Sarah murmurs.

Wandering off in their memories, the two women have a quiet conversation in Inupiaq, and I remember that they've been speaking English for me. There is a long silence, and then Sarah says quietly, "*Taiku*" (thank you).

I almost answer, for they've often thanked me for helping, but then Minnie replies, "One more time we come here—*taiku*."

I wake up to Minnie bustling around, starting the stove, making coffee. "Good morning," she smiles, mixing a bowl of hotcake batter.

Sarah ducks through the tent door. "No wind. Just right for seining." After a large breakfast, we do chores (which include checking the gillnets again) and get ready for the day's real work. Both boats are emptied out and the seine—200 feet of float-rigged fine mesh weighted with caribou horn and stones—is arranged in the center of Sarah's boat. As we sort and bag fish, a young bull moose trots along the bar across from camp. We consider going after it, but decide we have enough to do.

Two miles up the Kobuk, Shungnak Creek spills in from the north. We pull up and build a warming fire on the bar; the ground is still stiff with frost. Although we finished breakfast two hours ago, the women insist on eating. "You have to eat lots so you won't get tired," they say. Minnie wraps a whole pike in foil and roasts it on the coals. As it bubbles, we eat crackers, dried caribou meat, and seal oil washed down with hot tea.

There's another reason for waiting; Sarah and Minnie are watching the river, looking upstream and down for the telltale *miniq* (rise) of spawning whitefish. "If we don't put the net in the right place, it's just lots of work and no fish," Minnie says. The river bottom has to be smooth, snag free, and not too deep for the net. In this stretch of the river, there are several good places.

At first there's nothing; the river, 300 yards wide, is smooth and gray in the morning light. Then, just below the mouth of the creek, Sarah spots a rise, then another, and then we see dozens. The women point and speak excitedly. I don't need a translation. The roasted pike will have to wait.

We pole Sarah's boat downstream and beach just above the rising fish. Sarah passes me one end of the net, which is spread by a willow stick and attached to seventy-five feet of nylon rope. I stay on shore and anchor one end.

Working quickly and quietly, the women lay out the seine, Minnie poling while Sarah feeds the net over the side in a smooth arc. As soon as they reach shore, Minnie leaps out, leans all her weight against the rope at her end, and shouts, "Pull, pull! Real fast now!" As we heave in, hand over hand, Sarah poles back upstream along the outside edge of the net, thrashing the water as she goes to drive the fish toward shore, away from the net until the weights reach bottom and seal off escape. Panting, my arms burning, I dig in my heels and yank in the last two yards of line. Then I have the stick at the end of the seine, and start hauling on that.

"No, no! Too far! That's enough!" Sarah cries. "Tie it and go help her!"

I run two hitches around a drift log and sprint the fifty yards to Minnie, who has her end nearly in. "Look, we have fish!" she says. The curve of water before us is boiling with them—hundreds, no, thousands. I can feel them surging against the net, a heavy, vibrant pulse that jerks at my shoulders. At my feet, fish are throwing themselves ashore, flopping against my boots, and falling back into the maelstrom.

While I hang on, Minnie and Sarah secure the ends of the net, and our hands are free. Something big is churning the water against the floats. "Sheefish!" says Sarah. I wade out, grab the twenty pounder, and heave it onto the sand.

"Here," Minnie says, handing me a large washtub and some plastic gunnysacks. "Put the *kalusraak* in these." The women wade in ankle deep and start shoveling whitefish ashore with their hands. Most are *kaalgiks* (humpback whitefish) between one and two pounds, but there are a few *kausriluk* (broad whitefish), which are twice as large.

I set to work, grabbing the ten-inch, iridescent *kalusraak* two and four at a time and tossing them into the tub. I count 300 fish to a tubful, and empty the tub into a sack. The work is both hand-numbing and backbreaking, a constant blur of motion. Five tubs. Six. The fish seem endless. Minnie and Sarah are working on the hump-backs, skewering them through the cheeks on willow sticks they've cut nearby. When they have twenty fish, they knot the supple willow to form an easily handled wreath known as a "stick." "That's the way we always do it," Sarah says. Flushed from hard work in the cold air, she and Minnie both seem younger than I remember, almost girlish.

Eight tubs and two hours later, my hands are stiff and pale, soaked inside rubber gloves. My coveralls are smeared with blood and fish slime, damp with sweat. I stand upright to warm my fingers in my pockets, and nearly faint. My tongue seems thick, and I realize I'm shivering steadily. "Are you all right?" Minnie asks, looking up. "You should stop and rest. We'll build a fire and eat." She shows no sign of fatigue; neither does Sarah.

I take a deep breath and shake my head. "No, I'm fine," I say. "Let's finish."

We continue, gradually drawing in the net, freeing it from snags, scooping back escaping fish. At last we're down to a few hundred *kalusraak* and a dozen whitefish. Minnie snatches a fish bursting with roe, lifts it, and squeezes a stream of orange eggs into her mouth.

"Aarigaa!" she exclaims, her lips glistening, an egg stuck to her

cheek. Then she catches me watching her, and we both lower our eyes. "I'm sorry to eat *suvuks* like that in front of you," she says, embarrassed.

"No, no, it doesn't bother me," I reply, but I know she doesn't believe me. I can't find the words to tell her why I'm ashamed—it's not of her, but of my own squeamishness, of my own inability to seize the land and suck life from it as it wriggles in my hands.

The sun is settling to the south as we hoist the last fish into the boat. We make a final tally of our one seine haul—twelve tubs of *kalusraak*, thirty-four sticks of whitefish, two dozen grayling, and a twenty-pound sheefish—over four thousand fish, all from one haul. "Is this the most you've ever gotten in one seine?" I ask Minnie.

"Oh, no," she says with a shrug. "Lots more. A big boat like Nelson's, full to the top."

I shake my head. "Lots of work."

"That's what we want to do," Sarah says. "Work hard until the season is over."

The next morning is clear and sharply cold. "East wind," Minnie says. "You see that mountain—the one we call Old Man? It always tells us when stormy weather is coming."

"How soon?" I ask.

"Tomorrow," she says. The peak she points to, thirty miles off, is shrouded by low clouds. I nod, squint at the blue sky overhead, and decide—incorrectly—that the weather will hold for a few days.

We break camp and load the boats. The tent is emptied, the cache locked. "We won't come back this fall," Minnie says. The Black River camp will drift off to sleep with the land, and wait for another season.

Sarah's boat wallows against the bank, weighed down by nearly a ton of fish. Heaped to the gunwales, the *kaalgik* gleam like wet coins. The women add their camping gear to the pile, then climb in. Everything—boots, jackets, gas cans, seats—is coated with a sheen of dried slime and the sweet, pungent odor of whitefish.

From where I stand, the two women seem to be submerged to the waist in their treasure. "Will you be all right?" I ask.

"We'll travel slow," says Minnie. "Let the boys know we're coming."

When I gun my outboard, the boat rises sluggishly, weighed

down by a thousand pounds of fish, but finally reaches planing speed. Behind me, Minnie and Sarah are rounding the bend. Thirty miles from home, nearly awash with their load, they smile and wave like schoolgirls, complete in the promise of their moment.

I started hearing that teachers and preachers will come ever since I was small. Some real old good people knew about God and knew that the missionaries were coming, and it was true because Robert and Carrie Sams [sic] came. When Robert Sams came I had my first period; he came the second year after [when Edna was about sixteen and a half]. Robert and them came in a big ship. In 1897 they built the Friends Church in Kotzebue. Later they came to Noatak and had a little ebrulik *[sod house]; then they built the old mission.*

—from the autobiography of
Edna Hunnicutt, *The Eskimo Storyteller*,
by Edwin S. Hall, Jr.

Two Worlds, One Spirit

▲▲▲▲▲▲▲▲▲

A t one minute before nine on an October morning, this could be a junior high classroom anywhere in America. Students are sharpening pencils, sleepily digging in desks, or anticipating tonight's big game. The room has all the trappings of comfortable affluence—new carpeting, a bank of computers, art prints on the freshly painted walls. Behind my desk, I glance over lesson plans and take a last gulp of coffee.

"All right, folks, it's showtime. In your seats and Pageants books open to page 146. While we're getting set, who can tell me something about tropical rainforests?" My voice is lost in a roar from outside, and kids stand, craning their necks toward the windows. A snow machine strains by, pulling a heavily loaded sled.

"Man, Clarence get lots of caribous!"

"Hoohh, real big ones!"

"Sure wish I could go hunt."

I shake my head, then grin and join them at the window. "Okay, everyone, enough. Brazil, remember? Tricia, could you tell us . . ."

Outside, the expanse of arctic Alaska stretches to the horizon, distant mountains glowing blue and white in the low morning sun.

This is the Ambler School. So much for the one-room log cabin with a wood stove, the rows of fur-clad children reciting the alphabet. Although ninety-odd percent of Alaska is still a roadless wilderness of tiny villages adrift on an ocean of land, the trappings of today's technology and education arrived a decade ago and are here to stay—computers, standardized tests, and the latest instructional buzzwords.

But outside there's that sledload of caribou going by, and you'd discover scores of incongruities in a walk around Ambler, or any other village in the region. Satellite dishes next to cabins chinked with moss; racks of meat and drying animal skins by trim prefabricated houses; sled dogs and the latest high-tech snowmobiles, VCRs and outhouses; a tiny video arcade with a woodstove. It's as if you're viewing the aftermath of a violent collision between the past and present.

That image isn't so far from the truth. The modern age didn't so much advance on the Eskimos of the northwest arctic as it exploded over their heads like a dazzling firework. They've known schools for less than a century.

For two thousand years they lived as seminomadic hunter-gatherers, moving back and forth along the coast or up and down river valleys with the natural rhythm of seasons and animal migrations. The climate was harsh—snow in September, breakup in late May, and temperatures of forty, even seventy below. All their energy and ingenuity went into perfecting a technology of survival. Education for boys meant learning to hunt, travel, and make tools; girls learned to sew skins, cook and store food, and raise families. All their needs came from the land.

They spoke a language almost Shakespearean in its elegance and precision, and kept a rich oral tradition of myths, tales, family histories, and exploits. There was, though, no written language, or the need for one. Shamans, healers, and expert storytellers in each clan served as living archives, passing along all they knew to apprentices. The rest of the world was so remote that the name the Eskimos gave themselves, *Inupiat,* means "The Real People," or simply "The People." There were no others.

There was little change in the northwest arctic, even after white explorers appeared in the eighteenth and nineteenth centuries. Russian, English, or American, they stopped just long enough to trade and lend their names to places they passed.

Not until July 1897 did the first missionaries arrive—Robert and Carrie Samms and Edna Hunnicutt of the Friends (Quaker) Church. They had been recruited by the Eskimos of Kotzebue, who had grown impatient waiting for a mission to establish itself and had taken matters into their own hands, sending a delegation two thousand miles to the south in search of candidates. A converted Selawik man named Uyagaq had seen the good things missionaries had brought to the Yukon settlement of Unalakleet, and he convinced The People that life would be better and richer with spiritual instruction, medical care, and schools.

With Uyagaq's help as interpreter, the Samms built a mission. Sincere and energetic, they quickly won the respect and loyalty of many Eskimos—learning to speak Inupiaq, adopting local clothing and food, and immersing themselves in ministering to both the minds and bodies of their flock. Besides aiding Robert in his preaching and doctoring, the two women taught math and English, fed the children, and introduced the northwest arctic's first scholastic sport—ice skating.

Friends missions soon spread throughout the region, and there was a school at each. The Eskimos who had been living at scattered camps gravitated to these places, and villages were born—Kobuk, Shungnak, Kivalina, Deering, Buckland, Noatak, Noorvik. Trading posts followed, cementing the bond of place. Almost overnight, a nomadic people gave up one life for another.

Looking back, the willingness of The People to be shaped into something else is surprising, even disconcerting. Although they had their own unique culture firmly in place, they obviously wanted what the missionaries offered. One can only speculate whether knowledge, spiritual enlightenment, medical care, or trade was most important. Schools, though, were certainly a major attraction. In Kobuk there were so many eager learners that missionary-teacher James Geary opened a night school to relieve the pressure on his crammed facility.

Naturally, the main text was the Bible, and instruction, both in school and out, was aimed toward producing civilized Christians. What didn't fit in had to go. Some of the changes were welcome; the missionaries broke the hold of the *anjatkut* (shamans) and did away with harsh, often brutal taboos. But Eskimo drum dancing, too, was soon banned; the raw pagan power of the dances seemed threatening. Also, Christian marriages and funerals (even for those long united or long dead) were mandated. In some cases, people were sent out on the tundra with burlap sacks to gather the bones of their ancestors for "proper" burial.

It wasn't long before children were forbidden to speak their native tongue in school; English was the language of the Bible. Some elders recall being beaten for lapsing into Inupiaq, and school discipline in general was uncompromising. A piece of firewood was typical daily admission. Tardiness (a novel concept to a people without clocks or calendars) was punished; children judged too dirty were sometimes stripped and scrubbed on the spot. And yet they came of their own free will, to learn a strange new path and forget the only way they knew—a way remembered in a language they were forbidden to speak.

The transition was not without small but pointed acts of rebellion. In Noorvik, some disgruntled soul hurled a stick at the big outdoor clock in the meetinghouse tower, freezing the hands forever at 10:37 and putting a crimp in the local minister's punctuality program. In Kivalina a teacher tried to institute a spanking council, described by Friends historian Arthur Roberts: "All the bad boys in the school were led to the coal shed and a coal sack was put over the culprit's head so that the boy couldn't tell which member of the council was doing the spanking." Roberts adds, "This procedure didn't yield the expected results. The next year the teachers at Kivalina were Eskimo."

In the first quarter of the new century, the Friends minister-teacher program was gradually supplanted by the federal government's Bureau of Indian Affairs (BIA). At first the BIA gave just financial aid and supplies, but as the Friends found it harder and harder to find willing teachers, the government assumed more responsibility. Finally, in 1928 Superintendent of Education Sylvester Chance was forced out of office and replaced by non-Quaker George Morelander. He charged that the Friends had exerted an ideological stranglehold on the region's schools, regardless of the good they had done.

During the same period, the steady influx of white miners, missionaries, and traders led to the establishment of segregated schools—BIA or Friends schools for Natives, smaller, generally superior facilities for whites and children of mixed blood. Not until 1938 were local schools integrated, and even then, double standards lingered for thirty years. With whites in firm control of economy and government, and white culture the newly established norm, Eskimo schoolchildren found themselves on the outside looking in; after centuries spent curled in a cultural womb, success was suddenly redefined, and in terms they scarcely understood. Wealth was no longer something one gathered from the land and shared freely; the skills and values of their parents had been replaced by the foreign notions of discipline, punctuality, and frugality.

The BIA program evolved so that each village had a small primary and middle school, and Eskimos who wanted high school were shipped to centralized institutions as far off as Oregon and Oklahoma. Keeping families together wasn't an issue; education and acculturation were. This system remained in place from World War II through the 1960s, though some facilities were ceded to the state, which also built a centralized school in Kotzebue.

Then oil was discovered at Prudhoe Bay, and everything changed. The pipeline revenues started gushing in—hundreds of millions of dollars. The state of Alaska was suddenly wealthy beyond its wildest dreams. The Department of Education couldn't have avoided the deluge if it had wanted to.

The state could now afford to build a complete modern facility in each and every bush community—and in fact they had no choice. Maybe it was just coincidence, but the Alaska State Supreme Court ruled in 1976 that every child had a right to a complete education in his or her home village. Alaskan Natives had been lobbying steadily for local schools, but there had been no money, they'd been told. Now their suit, perfectly timed, appeared before the Court. The decision, known as the Hootch consent decree, cemented the state's commitment to decentralizing education—by building and maintaining a hundred small schools scattered across an area the size of the United States east of the Mississippi. The price tag would be one to three million per village, plus about a million a year to run each program. The logistics were staggering, but now the money was there. For the next five years, school construction proceeded all across the state.

What Ambler (population 250 in 1979) got was typical: a $1.5 million high school for less than fifty students, and the old state school renovated for the elementary. There was carpeting in every classroom, a new gym, a small mountain of equipment and supplies. Ten teachers were hired for 100 children, supported by a staff that included principal, cook, secretary, janitors, and aides. With almost unlimited funding and a fresh start, the eleven schools of the newly established Northwest Arctic Borough School District seemed destined for success.

It didn't take long for everyone to discover that education couldn't be bought. Some of the problems the district faced had been anticipated, but others were new and uniquely Alaskan. For one thing, the flashy new buildings had their share of bugs—faulty wiring, pipes that froze whenever the temperature got past 30 below (which was often), furnaces that wouldn't stay lit. Some of the gadgetry was just too complex or touchy for the arctic, and critical parts could take weeks to arrive. The newly installed village utility systems (also bought with oil money) were, if anything, less dependable. Power outages, sometimes as long as three weeks in the dark of winter, were a fact of life, and almost every village's water system failed due to poor design or maintenance.

At Noatak in 1981, where I first taught in Alaska, we tried to conduct classes by the light of faltering emergency generators in rooms so cold you could see your breath. Janitors had to haul water from ice holes in the local river; bathrooms were a nightmare of clogged toilets and old-fashioned honey buckets. Showers became a memory. It didn't happen all at once or everywhere, but as work crews scrambled to straighten out one site, another would go down.

Teacher housing ranged from sparse to spartan. The lucky ones wangled old prefabricated BIA quarters or rented one of the new federally funded Native housings. The stories of the less fortunate are legion. Running water and flush toilets were often an impossible dream. Conrad Gonzalez over in Buckland ended up in a converted packing crate; Brian McDermott lived in his classroom because his cabin's stove couldn't keep up with the frost coating the walls. My first year in Noatak I was so overrun by voles (robust arctic mice) that I took to hunting them indoors with a .22 pistol. I shot up to six a night for three months, and carved notches on a beam—126 by January. I ended up trading varmints for a bullet-riddled cabin and figured it was a bargain. I hadn't come up here to live in a trailer, anyway. All across the region, teachers making forty grand and more found themselves living in substandard shacks that often rented for staggering sums.

Groceries and supplies came in once or twice a week on scheduled small planes, or, in the short summer, on infrequent river barges. The village stores offered few choices at prices double or triple Outside rates. Teachers quickly learned to plan ahead and shop by mail for anything from chain saws to cheese, and to buy by the case or fifty-pound bag.

Teaching in these conditions, hundreds of miles from the nearest road that led anywhere, with four hours of subzero twilight in December, wasn't for everyone. Unsuspecting prospects came from the Lower 48, lured by a salary scale that topped out over sixty thousand. Some got out of the Cessna that had flown them in, took one look, and stepped back on the plane. Others lasted a few months and fled, pursued by rumors of breakdowns or suspicious behavior. One principal fled at Christmas with the school's payroll checks in his briefcase. The checks were sent back, but the man vanished. That same principal was later rehired by another bush district; people there understood how it could get. Here, as elsewhere in Alaska, teachers lasted an average of less than two years in a given village.

Most of the teachers who stayed on could be put into categories. There were the ones who hung on for the money by either gritting their teeth or becoming affable slackers. Often teaching couples in the upper end of the salary bracket, so-called "pipeliners," could gross over a hundred grand. In fifteen years they'd pay off the mortgage on their Arizona bee farm or Miami condo and retire.

Then there were professional teachers who practically lived and slept at the schools, and had few outside interests. These were older singles or serious career types with a family. Their world consisted of district-supplied living quarters, the adjacent school, and paths to the village store and post office. Two of these lifers could hold a school together—and sometimes did.

The majority of teachers, though, were young single men like me. Energetic but inexperienced, we'd been lured north by childhood dreams of Alaska, an independent streak, or pure eccentricity. We plunged into the job with the careless enthusiasm of youth and learned the hard way. Maybe the most severe hardship we found was a scarcity of eligible women—a crux that drove some away, and led others to seek mail-order brides. I ran a personal ad in the back of *Alaska* magazine, waded through three dozen replies, and came close.

Rounding out the District staff was a sprinkling of seasoned BIA veterans, local Eskimo teachers, hardcore outdoorsmen, adventurous single women, and those politely referred to as unstable.

When you threw a mixed staff of ten into a village halfway up an arctic river, anything could happen. Some groups proved naturally cohesive; others split into bitter factions. One bunch became so embroiled over rights to the school's washing machine that the district superintendent had to step in and threaten transfers for all. In another case, two teachers had to be pulled apart and restrained from mutual bloodletting on school time, in a ruckus over missing supplies.

The village people were sometimes more than spectators in these staff wars. Small towns anywhere thrive on rumors, and the teachers as outsiders were natural targets. A clash over student discipline or between personalities could lead to a one-way ticket out. Too, there were cultural misunderstandings, and some teachers were less than sensitive to Native values.

In rare instances, frustration disintegrated to the edge of violence. Things got so hot in one village that threats against teachers closed the school for a week. In another place a teacher packed a .45 as defense against his landlord—after he'd found himself looking down the wrong end of a hunting rifle. But here and elsewhere, triggers were never quite pulled, and school went on.

Caught in the middle of all this were the children. Given the heritage of the past century, the school district's shaky beginnings, and the ambiguous cultural context they faced, it's not surprising their performance was uneven. The missionaries had been rather successful in eradicating the Inupiaq language (few or no children now spoke it among themselves), but the English that replaced it was far from the language of their teachers. Instead, it was a polyglot. Labeled "village English" by some, it incorporated a few Inupiaq words into the framework of a limited English vocabulary, with grammar borrowed from both. Phrases like "I always never go there yet" meant something; the standard English of the teachers and their texts was somewhat more intelligible than Latin.

Standardized test scores (the SRA and ACT the district's yardstick then) were as low as you'd expect—with questions about fire engines, cows, and curbstones lost on children who'd never seen them. Many students scored in the bottom 10 percent of the national scales, and the district-wide average wasn't much better—around the twenty-fifth percentile. Teachers complained about lack of student motivation and home support. Parents complained that teachers were insensitive or ineffective.

The one area the Northwest Arctic Borough School District excelled in from the start was sports; in a matter of five years, the district established itself as a state power in cross-country running, skiing, and basketball. There were fewer cultural prejudices built into athletes.

Meanwhile, the school district, at last under local control, mandated that Inupiaq language and culture be taught to each and every child. Elders who remembered being tied to a chair for speaking

Eskimo were now hired to undo the previous eighty years. The results, like those in all other classes, were decidedly mixed. Some teenagers sneered at "Eskimo jive," while others, especially the younger ones, learned rapidly. Still, you learn the language you hear at home, and most parents, out of force of the habits instilled by the missionaries, still spoke English to their children.

Most of this Inupiaq cultural renaissance was applauded, but when it came to teaching drum dancing in the schools, the protests came from an unlikely source: Eskimo elders. Many saw it as a revival of shamanism and a token of disrespect to them, God, and church; letters were written, protests filed, and that was the end of drum dancing in most villages.

With the Northwest Arctic Borough School District now entering its thirteenth year, The People find themselves still learning, still adapting to a changing environment. Oil money has dwindled with world prices, and the promise of revenues from the region's Red Dog mine, one of the largest lead-zinc deposits anywhere, is, at best, a few years down the road. As budgets have been slashed, villages that once had ten teachers find themselves with six, and every phase of education—books, administration, maintenance, sports, course offerings—has been rolled back. Schools that once had more money than they could spend sometimes run short of basic needs like paper.

And yet the quality of education continues to improve, in spite of—or perhaps in part because of—the new austerity. Everyone's been forced to make more out of less.

As the region and district have grown, more teachers are seasoned veterans of the Alaskan bush, and many of the "pipeliners" have been weeded out. The once-intoxicating air of youthful enthusiasm and almost desperate adventure seems to have given way to quiet competence—to the sorrow of some, who reminisce about the good old days (not so long ago) when someone deposited a severed moosehead on the superintendent's doorstep to illustrate a point, and drunken teachers fired a shotgun salute to welcome their new principal.

Student achievement has climbed steadily, if not dramatically, perhaps as a result of acculturation (including television) and more effective instruction. Standardized test scores now average ten points higher than a decade ago—though that average still ranks under the fiftieth percentile nationally—and the number of students performing at top levels has soared. Northwest arctic schools have added a handful of statewide academic awards to match their athletic titles; some students are at last finding success in college. Several have returned to become teachers, and there is the promise of more to come.

Still, staggering problems remain—some educational, some social. Money is tighter than ever; students are still at a cultural disadvantage; teacher turnover is still high; alcohol abuse affects a majority of households. The future can only promise more difficulties, some as yet unseen. Perhaps the greatest challenge is, to quote the slogan on a local poster, to "walk in two worlds with one spirit"—to hunt caribou and then sit down at a computer, or sew mukluks and later balance a checkbook—to remain Inupiat in a world of modern technology. The odds against striking such a balance are steep; but then, thousands of arctic winters have bred into The People a talent for survival. They may just pull it off.

*After walking along the hill they decided to go
down to the creek in a timbered country, and all of
a sudden in a small clearing they got real close to
a bear with two small cubs. The mother bear
caught their scent so she went to the side of the two
cubs and put them behind her to protect them.
And so the man got his spear ready and said to the
bear, "So we are going to protect our young ones,
is that it?"*

*Well, the bear could not talk but she got real
curious. The boys had already climbed a big birch
and were watching to see what their dad would do
with the bear. They had not seen their dad kill a
bear before so they were watching closely every
move he made. Finally he walked toward the bear,
and all of a sudden the bear jumped at him, but
the man jumped aside to the right and as the bear
was passing he poked the point of the spear into the
bear's chest. Again the bear attacked so the man
jumped aside again and gave the bear another hit
on the side. The bear could not charge a third
time. It was bleeding and dying. The man then
chased the young cubs and killed them too, so there
were three bears for a good supper.*

—James Wells, *Ipani Eskimos*

My Last Grizzly

△△△△△△△△△

I love bears, and I have killed them: two grizzlies and two blacks in the past twelve years. I've also helped to kill two other grizzlies. I could say I needed them for food, but I didn't eat them; I could claim self-defense, but that would be a lie—for in all cases, I set out with the idea of killing a bear. I did take away hides for myself, and meat to share with my Eskimo friends, but utility has little to do with it. There is a picture of me with my first grizzly. I had it blown up to eight by ten, and I set it on the shelf next to my collection of skulls.

The date was May 7, 1982. The bear is lying on one side, head angling toward the camera. He is a large but not especially pretty specimen, a mature boar with thick fur and hooked claws. His head and shoulders are brushed with silver, the legs and paws so dark they seem almost black. The bear's mouth is sagging open, and his small eyes are closed. His head lies in a pool of frozen blood. He died on the windswept ice of a small lake; the blood ran from his nose and mouth and froze around him as he died. The bear's side, too, is covered with a sheen of frozen blood. If this were a war movie, you'd complain that it looks fake. If you moved the 600-pound carcass, you'd see a great deal more blood underneath. The bear died hard. It took ten shots from two rifles to kill him.

I'm on the right side of the photo, squatting behind the bear's shoulder with my rifle pointing skyward. What I like best about this picture is my face. You can tell I was younger then, though my skin is weathered from days of snowmobiling in subzero cold. If you looked quickly, you'd see a happy young man. My teeth are white, and my eyes are crinkled slits above high cheekbones. But look at the eyes.

53

Look at the corners of the mouth. I'm sure I thought I was smiling. Years later I look back at myself and wonder what I've learned. Around the two figures in the photo, the foreground and background are without form or depth, a dreamlike blur anchored only by the hard pool of blood.

I came to Alaska because of bears. Bears, Alaska, Alaska, bears. The two were the same to me. I was afraid of bears then, so afraid I couldn't ignore their existence. It seemed I had no choice but to go and find exactly what it was that I feared.

The first Alaskan grizzly I saw made a lasting impression on me, and he wasn't even alive. It was the enormous stuffed bear at the University of Alaska museum in Fairbanks. He stands upright in a glass case just inside the door. I had to lean back to focus on his head, eleven feet off the floor. The plaque gave his live weight at 1,200 pounds. His front legs, at the bicep, were nearly as big around as my torso. He wasn't mounted like a Hollywood bear, snarling, paws raised. Instead, he stood in what I'd later recognize as a classic grizzly pose: leaning forward, round-shouldered, squinting like an elderly gentleman, a vaguely puzzled expression on his face. I looked, and knew that a gun would be useless. And yet he was there, dead. A hunter had killed him. I stood there for half an hour, shaking my head, imagining that thing rising out of the brush twenty feet away.

Two weeks later on the Kobuk River, I saw my first wild grizzly. My traveling partner Peter Torres and I were drifting downstream in a canoe just above the Maniilaq River. The bear was lying on a gravel bar fifty yards off, and at first he seemed just another stump. Then the head raised. His fur was matted with rain, and his small eyes glittered as he turned. He saw us at about the same time we saw him, and he burst into motion, bounding off into the willows as if a huge spring were uncoiling inside his chest. There had been no time to be afraid.

It was a month before we saw another grizzly, though we were traveling through prime bear country and looking hard. We saw a few black bears, but only grizzlies would do now. On the Noatak River late one summer evening, as we floated with the current, we saw one. He was lying on a high cutbank, front paws spread, grazing on blueberry bushes. A big silver-blond male, he looked as peaceful as a grazing cow. As we drifted down on him—fifty yards, then thirty—he saw us.

Being nearsighted like all bears, maybe he wasn't sure what we were, but he slid to his feet and began to slink down the bank, stalking us. I backwatered with my paddle, and at my motion the bear leaped, turned in midair, and vanished over the bank.

Feeling brave, we made camp a half mile below, on the same side of the river. We stacked our plates to clatter us awake and slept with a loaded .44 Magnum pistol between us. Later on, a hunting guide told me that if I wanted to carry a .44 for bear protection, I'd better file off the front sight. Why, I asked. So it won't hurt so much when the bear shoves it up your ass, he said.

Over the next five years I asked questions about bear attacks. I listened to trappers, Eskimos, state troopers, game wardens, biologists, hikers, and hunters. I heard a rumor that so-and-so's uncle had been torn apart and eaten by a grizzly years ago, leaving nothing but a booted foot; when I followed it up, I was told I was mistaken. I heard about hunters being charged, but then I found out the bear had been wounded first, or had been chased with a snow machine. A park service ranger got bowled over by a sow with cubs, and yet she ended up more shaken than hurt. A geologist was charged and grabbed by the arm, but all he got were some nasty punctures that needed sewing. There are plenty of narrow escapes, but in the history of the northwest arctic, there seemed to be only one authentic case of a grizzly killing a man—an Eskimo hunter who was mauled by a wounded bear he was tracking, and later died of his injuries. You could hardly blame the bear.

Of course, the northwest arctic is a fragment of the grizzly's North American range, and what's true here doesn't necessarily hold for other places. Where they are not shot at, as in Denali Park, bears show little fear of man, which is probably their natural condition.

One reason for the rarity of bear trouble in the northwest arctic is simple demographics; people are fairly scarce, if conspicuous. Seven thousand humans inhabit an area roughly the size of Maine—and more than half live in Kotzebue, on the coast. Bears can be nearly invisible, even when they're much around. Bear sign is almost everywhere in the western Brooks Range, especially along rivers and streams and on brushy slopes: the distinctive pigeon-toed prints, rear feet almost human, front paws short, broad, and long-clawed; the piles of droppings; mounds of soil where they've dug for roots or ground squirrels; spruce trees with the bark clawed higher than a man can reach, long gold-tinted hairs caught in the resin. Along salmon sloughs and through narrow passes, there are beaten trails, often a series of circular depressions where generations of bears have stepped in the same measured stride. And yet seeing an arctic grizzly up close is an event, unless you're either lucky or skillful. Besides being shy around humans, bears are largely nocturnal. Much of the day they sleep in creek bottoms or high on brushy slopes, their coats blending into the landscape.

Even in the northwest arctic, bears don't always run. A big male, especially, may choose to be aggressive. The bear senses trespassers on his turf. His eyesight isn't the best, though he seems to pick up movement well, and he can spot aberrations in the landscape. Naturally he runs at the animal in question. If it's another bear, he has to defend his territory. If it's some prey animal, like a crippled caribou or a lost moose calf, he naturally would like to know. But what if the trespasser is neither prey nor competitor, and doesn't respond properly? What if the intruder just stands there?

Dave Rue of Ambler, a good outdoorsman and one of the region's top bush pilots, was on a fall sheep hunt in the Maiumerak Mountains a few years ago. While hiking, he and his partner spotted a big grizzly on a hillside a quarter mile off. The bear saw their movement, and came charging right for them. They got ready to shoot, but held off and stood their ground. The bear kept coming, pausing to rise on his haunches and peer at them, then dropping down and bounding on. When it got within fifty yards, Dave and his friend braced. As they raised their rifles, the bear caught their scent. Just as quickly as he'd come, he was gone.

"He was one big son of a bitch," Dave told me, "and he looked like business there for a while." I asked him what the bear looked like. Was it a blond animal, close to nine feet with a dark, almost black face? This standard hunting measurement is the greatest length and width of a stretched hide divided by two. Exactly where had the bear been? Sure enough, I knew him. Noatak Eskimos who trapped the area called him Blondie, but my friend Bert and I had a less glamorous name. We'd had a scrape with him, just two weeks before Dave's. The bear had appeared across from camp just before dusk, a speck of glistening movement in the willows. We'd forded the stream and stalked him just to see what he was up to, but he'd spotted us at about a hundred yards, and had begun a stalk of his own. We lost sight of him—an uncomfortable sensation at dusk in a snow shower—and then he'd risen sixty yards away, bluffed a charge, winded us, and bounded off, his huge rump pulsing with muscle and fat. This bear was the largest and finest we'd ever seen, so naturally we called him Shitface, as a way of bringing him down to our level. He might not have survived either encounter had the men been more trigger happy, or had they wanted to kill a bear. As it is, I've found his tracks several times since, and spotted him again on that same gravel bar, five years after he might have died in a "bear attack." I worry about him, though. Sooner or later Shitface is bound to run out of luck because he does too good a job of being a bear. He's the first grizzly I thought of as a friend, someone whose country I visited as an uninvited guest. I'd like to think of him always being there, serving notice to trespassers in his little valley.

Talking to some German hikers, I heard about a less fortunate bear. The two young men were on the trip of their lifetime, backpacking through the hills near Noatak. They had a gun with them for protection—a surplus Mauser with military hardpoint ammunition—the wrong bullets for a big animal. They weren't hunters, nor good shots. They'd never seen a wild bear. A big grizzly had come at them, and they'd started shooting at a hundred yards. They hit him twice, they were sure, but he didn't drop. He turned and ran, and the two Germans went on their way, feeling lucky to be alive. They were excited about it when they told me. I thought of the bear, dying slowly on a hillside because his message had been misunderstood. There was no use telling the Germans anything. They had the story they'd come for, something to tell their grandchildren someday.

Despite all the pressure from humans, state biologists believe more brown/grizzly bears (now considered two names for the same species, *Ursus arctos*) live in Alaska than in 1900. Some hunters and biologists think the population is higher than it would be if there were no hunting allowed at all. This claim seems absurd, but it's based on field research and sound reasoning. It turns out that grizzlies have their own system of population control. Simply put, big bears eat smaller bears—cannibalism. The big males, bears like Shitface, apparently catch and kill smaller bears whenever they can. Cubs and subadults newly on their own are the ones most often eaten. They wander into a dominant male's territory and become fair game. Fiercely maternal as she is, a sow may not be able to save all of her two or three cubs from a male twice her weight. If one is snatched, she retreats with the others. I saw cannibalism for myself in August 1984, on the edge of Shitface's territory. My two partners and I rounded a bend and spotted a carcass on the gravel. I thought it was a young moose or a caribou, but it turned out to be a young female grizzly, maybe four years old. Her neck had been broken by a single bite, and her hindquarters and entrails—the most nutritious parts of her—had been eaten. There was still uncoagulated blood at her nostrils. The dead bear seemed to have been healthy; she had simply been ambushed or chased into the water by a much larger bear, one who might still be lurking in the willows twenty yards away. We decided it was time to leave.

Was Shitface the killer? There's a good chance he was. In any Brooks Range valley, there aren't too many big bears, and the kill was just five miles from his home base. If Shitface was the one, I don't like him any less—but it keeps me from being too sentimental about him. He's a bear. A killer, like me.

The traditional Inupiat attached great spiritual significance to the grizzly, whom they called *aklaq*. While they considered the black bear to be somewhat of a dimwit, they respected and feared the grizzly above all other animals. If a hunter killed one, the skin became the door of his house, and whoever entered was notified of the man's bravery and skill. Considering how bears were hunted in the days before firearms, such a door was no idle boast. A hunter would stalk a bear with a stout bone-tipped spear, or wait in ambush under a cutbank. When the surprised animal would rear up to get a better look at his attacker, the man would dart under the front paws, moving in from the right (since bears are said to be left-handed) and plant his spear on the ground, angling up and inward. As the bear came down to crush the man, he impaled himself. The hunter would dive out of the way and wait for the bear to thrash out his life, and finish him with another spear if needed.

Another way to get a bear would be to find a winter den— identified by the glazed breathing hole on a south-facing, well-drained hillside—and enter it by digging. The Inupiat say that a bear will not fight in his den. The hunter would either kill the bear inside with his spear, or drive the bear out into an ambush of waiting hunters. A more prudent method was to probe through the breathing hole with a long spear. When rifles came into use around the turn of the century, the same methods were used, with the rifle substituted for a spear.

Once a bear was killed, there were rules of spiritual etiquette which were strictly followed. The lower jaw was never detached, and a certain small piece of cartilage known as "the worm" was cut from the underside of his tongue and impaled on a willow; the head was always left in the field, either buried or impaled on a small spruce. The brain was never eaten. These acts assured that the bear's spirit would not molest the hunter, and that it would be born again. Although the old ways are fading out, most hunters still observe at least some of these traditions. I've never seen an Eskimo bring a bear's head into town.

The traditional reverence for grizzlies is easy to understand. They are the largest, strongest, and along with wolves and wolverines, the most intelligent creatures in a huge landscape. They have individual personalities, as we understand them—they lose their tempers, they play, show affection, and suffer from insatiable curiosity. Early hunters looked at bears and saw, perhaps, a reflection of themselves, cast in godlike proportions.

In April 1981, a year before I killed my first grizzly—the one in the photo—my friend Tove Jensen and I were riding near the headwaters of the Hunt River when I spotted a big boar grizzly bounding up a steep slope about 500 feet above us. I figured we'd spooked him, and that he'd keep going over the ridge. But at the top he stopped, turned, lowered his shoulder, and tumbled head over heels downhill, gaining speed in his own small avalanche. Then he dug in his paws, flipped upright, shook himself, and raced back to the top. He rolled down again, and once more. Finally he grew bored with the game and batted chunks of hard snow into the air, swatting them to powder. All the time, though, he kept a curious, careful eye on us. As Tove and I watched through binoculars, we saw him lie down, rest his chin on one paw in a classic thinking pose, and regard us, head cocking back and forth.

Watching that bear was like looking into a mirror. I decided I wasn't really on a bear hunt, though I'd come a hundred miles with a loaded rifle. I'd have to wait another year to find another bear that seemed less human.

April 14, 1985. I don't have to look at a calendar. It was the day before spring bear season opened. Norma (my companion for two years) and I were out scouting for dens, twenty miles into the Kipmiksots. We worked up a steep draw, our machines straining through deep powder. The sun was warm, though the air couldn't have been much above zero. The draw widened into a sheltered creek valley, the mountains rising sharply on three sides. A pair of wolf tracks wound through the willows on the valley floor, shining in the fresh snow. A band of caribou climbed over the rim and were gone. Even through dark glasses, the light was dazzling.

Norma signaled. I followed her point up the valley and there it was: a freshly dug out bear den, a trail emerging. Fifty yards away we pulled up. A big male, judging from the tracks, had come out in the last day. He'd dug out through the den roof, creating a deep, narrow trench about fifteen feet into the slope, open at one end. We couldn't see all the way in, but the first few feet seemed empty. At the mouth lay a huge mound of soil, rock, and willow, untouched by yesterday's dusting of snow. The only trail we could see led out, with nothing returning.

Norma roared ahead on her old Polaris, too excited to hear my bad joke about knocking first. I didn't think much about it, but as she dismounted twenty feet above the trench and moved in, camera in hand, I somehow knew: *he's still in there.* I gunned my machine up the slope, waving her off, cutting four feet from the edge of the hole. A snarling head erupted from the ground, and a paw hooked out at me. The roar was drowned out by the engine, but I didn't have to hear it. The bear was thrashing up the pit wall, jaws snapping, paws working cat-quick.

Norma stumbled backward and fell. This is it, I thought. He's going to be on us. The world slowed into bright slow motion. Just like a movie, I remember thinking. Could I turn him with my .22? Ten shots from a bird gun? No chance. Norma reached her machine and gunned it, spinning the track. Stuck. "You're not going to make it," I shouted as I pulled up and dragged her on behind me. I didn't look back. The bear had to be five feet behind. I braced almost calmly for the slamming impact, the hot breath, the teeth.

When we did look, the bear was already a hundred yards off and moving fast in the opposite direction. He'd charged out of the den entrance and kept going downhill. He'd had us both dead and let us go. He was a monster for an arctic grizzly—at least 600 pounds, fresh out of the den. At his fall prime he might top 800. A head the size of a TV set, I thought, then shook off the idiotic comparison. He wasn't a television set, or a movie. He was as real as the scar down his snout. He'd been ten feet away.

Once we'd calmed down enough, we followed him. There didn't seem to be any choice. By the time we caught up, he'd already dug a shallow hole in the creek bottom a quarter mile away, apparently a substitute den. He wanted to go back to the way things had been before we'd blundered in. We watched for half an hour and he ignored us, digging, tearing up brush and gouts of snow. I ran my machine down the hill and he charged, then turned as I pulled away. As long as we gave him a hundred yards, he wouldn't even look up. If we got too close, he thrashed the willows, chopped his jaws, and put on a rush. After an hour we left him, still digging. Three days later we returned, but blowing snow had covered his trail and sifted into the empty den.

May 10, 1986. A year later. 2:00 A.M. I'm alone on my battered Arctic Cat, twenty-five miles back in the Kipmiksots. In the past few weeks I've made a dozen trips, covering hundreds of miles with my machine, hundreds more with my eyes. I'm looking for a bear, a particular bear. I know where he denned last year, and I know what he looks like: a huge brown male with a scar on his snout. If you want an explanation for exactly why I'm hunting him, I don't have one, even for myself. An old-time Eskimo shaman (if there were any left) might say I'm looking for my *kila*, my animal helping spirit, so that he might give himself to me and make me strong. But this isn't enough; in fact, it's evasion. The part of me that knows the truth looks down bitterly and hopes for failure as the rest pushes on. Fear flutters in my gut, but I can no longer pretend it's of anything external.

The last few days have been warm; the spring thaw is right on schedule. The Noatak valley is a luminescent patchwork of brown and fading white. Even in the cool evening half light, the going is slushy and the creeks run with overflow. Once above 2,000 feet, though, the snow is solid, and the wind stings my face as I ride into it. I travel the ridgelines and drop into the same little creek valley, though I know he wouldn't den there again. I recognize the spot, but it's umarked, drifted in. That was another year. Gone, like Norma, whom I loved and harmed. I've been hunting hard all spring to keep away from the village, from the empty cabin, from another man's wife. Hunting hard, but only for one certain bear, as if his soul could somehow save mine. All failures merge into one, and become the thing I chase. *Is this how I repay him?*

It's been four weeks of looking, and the season will be done tomorrow, or the next warm day after that—collapsed inward, lost. I've crossed two bear trails tonight, and halfheartedly followed each one, knowing they weren't what I was after. One trail led to a winter killed caribou. All that was left were a few bone shards, trampled snow, hair, and mounds of scat. I lost the other trail in windrift.

I haven't slept in twenty-eight hours. The light throws all internal clocks off. Even now it's not truly dark; the light is gray and flat, faint, but enough. My fuel gauge shows just over half a tank. I'll cut across the mountain into the next watershed, ride along the creek for a few miles, then loop home. *Am I discouraged or relieved?* He'll be safe from me if he can last another two hours.

I bang across a stretch of rock-hard drifts and then a patch of bare tundra, and finally drop down into the creek. I know it well. Four years ago I shot my first grizzly here. It's good denning country, and big bears seem to favor it. A light snow is falling, tiny flakes like dust. The heavy ache of fatigue sickness is setting in, and my eyes play tricks on me. I look again, straining against the near whiteout of snow on snow. No depth perception. But yes, that's a bear trail before me. I've been riding right over it, not seeing. I stop and dismount, run my fingers over the prints. Steaming fresh—no snow in them yet, the outlines sharp but feather soft. The rear foot is over twelve inches long, eight wide. It's him, and he's less than five minutes ahead. I unsling my rifle and check the magazine. *Why pretend the odds are equal?*

I ride slowly, quietly as I can, the gun across my lap. The wind is in my face, and the snow muffles the machine's rattle. I leave the creek, clear a low rise, and there he is, the dark, wide rump shuffling along, less than 200 yards off, bigger than I remembered. He can't see me, hasn't smelled me, must not have heard. *Is he deaf?* I swing my rifle up, brace off my seat. The crosshairs fix on his rolling shoulder hump. The best way to put him down fast is with a spine shot. I take a deep breath, let half out, and touch the trigger.

Whump. A hit, but I've missed the spine. He lurches into a heavy-footed lope. I work the bolt and aim again. He staggers and turns toward me, charges. He's coming in, head low, determined, moving on instinct. Another shot and he's dead on his feet, but still coming, mouth open, spraying blood. He goes down on the fourth round, biting at his chest as if his own failing body is the enemy. Thirty yards away, I can hear his last breath sigh out: resignation, disappointment. All these seasons have come to this.

The gun slides from my gloved hands. I rock back and forth, crying as if he were my brother, the valley quiet and white with new snow.

Sometimes I don't know about you white people.

—Clarence Wood

Arctic Heroes

△△△△△△△△△

Deep in the Schwatka Mountains of the western Brooks Range, at the divide between the Kobuk and Noatak, is a small creek named Kavachuraq on the USGS map. Draining north into the Noatak, it's hardly distinguishable from any of a dozen streams in the area, except that it has an Eskimo name not yet lost in time. This is limestone canyon country—gray peaks of mineral-streaked, crumbling rock, ravines five hundred feet deep, and naked headwalls brushing against clouds. Snowdrifts lie in shadows where the sun never reaches, even at the height of arctic summer. It's a sparse, hungry land where lichens struggle for a foothold; you could imagine yourself in the mountain deserts of Mexico or North Africa if not for the grimy patches of snow.

There would be little reason for man or animal ever to visit the Kavachuraq, except that it offers a small, steep pass rising from the headwaters of the Ambler River into the Noatak drainage. Eskimo hunters and the caribou they followed used it over the centuries, and, later, bush pilots discovered it as a way to slide through the mountains when clouds were low. The caribou marked the trail with their bleached antlers, the Inupiat with scattered artifacts, and the pilots left their mark in turn. Just below the rim of the pass lies the wreck of a Norseman floatplane, the rusting airframe twisted by impact and fire. I've visited the place twice, drawn by the story that became, indirectly, a part of my life.

It's the summer of 1957. A Fairbanks prospector named Chuck Herbert, his son, and a young Eskimo man, Tommy Douglas, are setting out on a trip into the upper Noatak. Tommy claims he can lead them to a rich gold strike somewhere in the mountains above Midas Creek. In Kotzebue they charter a Wein Airlines Norseman, a big, slow, radial-engine floatplane. Ed Batten is the pilot, well-known and respected in the region. They load grub, prospecting tools, and camping gear into the Norseman, and fly east up the Kobuk River.

At the Ambler they turn north, following the ever-narrowing valley. The ceiling is lowering, but they keep on. The first pass, Natmaktugiaq, is closed, and the pilot decides to try another, Kavachuraq. It is, after all, a two-hour flight back to Kotzebue, an expensive charter for nothing. To fly where Batten can see, they are below the approaching headwall of the pass, hemmed in by gray rock a hundred yards off each wingtip, the dead-white clouds just overhead, the canyon floor below. Rounding the bend, they can see the pass, and there seems to be enough room to squeeze over. Further along, the ceiling should improve.

Then they're caught in the downdraft, the stream of cold air falling from the higher Noatak valley into the canyon. Batten pulls back on the controls, but the loaded Norseman responds sluggishly. Time compresses into heartbeats: full throttle, the big radial engine howling, the pilot willing the plane to rise, the passengers throwing out prayers as if they were sandbags. It's not enough. Aimed for the lowest point, the headwall rushing up, no room to turn, Batten yanks the nose up into a stall just as the plane slams in. Crushed by the buckled airframe and the engine, the pilot dies instantly in his seat. The fuselage folds back, gashed open, spilling the prospectors' gear over the slope. Fuel pouring from a ruptured wing tank catches a spark and ignites. Tommy Douglas, a leg mangled, somehow manages to pull Herbert, who is stunned and badly injured, clear, and then goes back for Herbert's son. The three huddle at the top of the pass, only forty yards above the wreck, as the plane burns. A day later, they are found and rescued by a searching helicopter, part of a geological survey crew working the area.

Thirty years later there is still the tortured airframe, one intact float, a jumble of heat-fused gear, blobs of aluminum, and scraps of rotten yellow fabric fluttering in the wind. Under the pilot's seat, there is a pair of shattered aviator's glasses. Human visitors are few, maybe a handful of geologists and backpackers over the years. But there have been others: a shard of aluminum, punctured by a grizzly's tooth;

clawmarks along the float; a beaten bear path, each saucer-shaped footmark distinct, leading from the pass and down the gully toward the canyon floor. Generations of bears have visited the wreck, occasionally gnawing and sniffing at the strange skeleton that lies in their path. But now, at dusk, there is no sign of life, and the ringing silence is broken only by the white noise of water far below.

I was two years old and far away at the time, but the crash started a chain of events that, twenty-two years later, would brush against me and change my life. Tommy Douglas lost his leg in the wreck, but won an insurance settlement from Wein Airlines. An enterprising man, he used part of the money to start a trading post in the newly established village of Ambler, and hobbled about for a time as a storekeeper on his wooden leg. Then he heard a call into the ministry, and became a Friends Church pastor, known across the region for his inspired evangelical preaching. A Dutch big game guide new to the area, Erik VanVeenen, bought out the languishing Douglas Trading Post in 1977 to use as a bunkhouse for his clients, and, after figuring the angles, decided there was money to be made running a village store on the side. This meant he needed a store manager, someone reliable and competent, with somewhat of a head on his shoulders but definitely malleable. In his eyes, someone definitely white, definitely not of the village.

He'd gone through at least two flunkies when Peter Torres and I sauntered into Ambler Trading on July 5, 1979, decked out in surplus camouflage, dark glasses, and two weeks' stubble. I'd been in Alaska for less than a month, and was fully aware of my leading role in an epic adventure. Maybe I'd read too much Jack London as a kid, or maybe it was the Hemingway later on, but somewhere along the line I'd decided that at least part of my life should be shaped like a '40s matinee. I knew who I was—a stranger with quiet, slightly dangerous eyes and a shrouded past, the kind men notice and women watch. I'm not sure who Peter was busy being, but it's safe to say that we were both Arctic Heroes.

"What's this, an invasion?" Erik VanVeenen looked up from his folding chair, pale eyes amused behind his wire-rim glasses. Before him was a half case of bruised nectarines that he was busily attacking with a pocket knife, cutting out soft spots and wolfing them down, one after another. Juice dribbled down his chin and he wiped it away, then seized another fruit. The sign said fifty cents each.

"No one will buy them anyhow like this. They'll just spoil. What brings you to Ambler?" The store was a chaos of gray steel shelving stacked to the low ceiling, crammed to overflowing with canned goods, gloves, radios, chain saws, a gun rack behind the cluttered counter, cases of pop stacked in the narrow aisles. Coke was dollar a can, and a small can of peaches a dollar twenty. It was the only game in town.

After ten days of running the Kobuk River and walking in the hills, we were ready to tell someone—anyone—about what we'd done and seen so far: the canoe almost swamping at the mouth of the Kobuk canyon; a pistol-waving standoff with a black bear at midnight; gold panning at the Reed River; the grizzly we'd jumped off a moose kill. We'd been hoping for something on which to carve the myths of our lives, and we'd found it.

But we'd also seen the trash piles at Eskimo fish camps, found geologists' stakes and benchmarks on our explorations of unnamed mountains, and our images were tarnishing steadily as we headed downriver past the first three Kobuk villages. Two more lay ahead. Floating Pepsi cans weren't included in our version of wilderness, and the mountains were receding as the valley's floodplain widened. Two hundred miles of the same faced us downstream.

Consulting a pocket guidebook to Alaskan rivers and our pile of survey maps, we elected to hang a right on the Ambler River, paddle fifteen miles upstream to the mouth of the Redstone, cutting into the heart of the western Brooks Range. Forty more miles up the Redstone was Ivishak Pass, a traditional Eskimo winter route (said the book) rising into the Noatak drainage. There'd be an eight-mile portage, then on down the Noatak three hundred miles to Kotzebue and the coast. Of course, we kept the book out of sight when we mentioned the idea to anyone.

"Been done before," Erik cheerfully informed us. "Read Sepp Weber's book, eh? How about straight up the Ambler?" A sly look stole across his face, a look I'd get to know too well.

"Tell you what. I've got a bit of shovel work to do on my new store's foundation. Give me a hand and I'll fly you up to look over the route. Let's see that map."

It turned out there was more than a bit of shovel work. There were forty piling holes to be dug, each four feet deep in half-frozen sand. It was hot work in the streaming sunlight of 10:00 P.M., draped in whining hordes of mosquitoes. The new building would be by far the largest structure in Ambler except for the brand-new school, and Erik planned to build most of it himself. He envisioned a modern supermarket in the arctic, fresh produce and a bank of freezers, luxurious living quarters upstairs. By the time we finished the thirtieth hole, two days and a backache later, I was hired as manager of the operation—to be effective upon my return from the Noatak. Peter, with his year of experience in Barrow, was offered the job first, but he'd had his fill of the north and was heading back to Maine. Looking back, I suspect he listened harder to the warning bells jangling in his head.

At least one of those bells had been set off by our first five minutes in Ambler, on the 200-yard walk up from the landing to the store. We'd beached the canoe and were rubbernecking along when a young Eskimo man scrambled by, panic in his eyes.

"You guys better run, he's coming!"

"Who, what, what's going on? Hey, wait!"

"Buddy! Sniffing gas again. He got machete!" And he was gone up the hill like a rabbit. Later I'd find that we'd just met Enoch Harding, the town constable of the moment. Buddy was his younger brother. The next likely official help would be Kotzebue, the state troopers, 130 miles away, an hour by air. We ducked into Ambler Trading and met Erik instead, and Buddy took his machete elsewhere.

The next day we found Cleveland Trading, a tiny Native store set up in the front room of a house. It was just as disorganized as Erik's, but the shelves were more sparse.

"Hello, white men! What you figure?" We met old Mark Cleveland, Erik's Eskimo counterpart. He was just as garrulous, just as sly, but clearly the white storekeeper's business and ideological rival. It took him no less time to find why we were in town. We were happy to tell him our story.

"They call that pass Natmaktugiaq. You know what that means, white men? 'Place to pack over.' Long ago they name it because too steep for dogsled. They have to carry their stuff up and down. Way too steep for kayak. You go Ivishak! Good trail, not so far over the mountains. Other white men go that way, couple years ago. Nobody ever go up Natmaktugiaq with kayak." Mark was waxing eloquent, apparently performing for himself as well as for us, conscious of the dramatic potential before him.

And so we were committed to Natmaktugiaq, drawn by its apparent impossibility. Mark's exasperated benediction, "Crazy white men!" rung pleasantly in our ears. We were Arctic Heroes again.

Erik flew us up the Ambler River late that evening. His plane, a Maule M-5 Lunar Rocket according to the logo on the tail, looked like a Piper Cub on steroids—stocky, unelegant, bristling with horsepower. Our introduction to Erik as a pilot was memorable; he flew the way the plane looked. It would take me a few years of flying with lesser, saner pilots to fully appreciate—and retroactively fear—what Erik could and would do with that Maule. But even in the bliss of partial ignorance, being his passenger was far from a casual pastime. Seeing what he thought was a bear, he veered into a bank approaching ninety degrees, so we found ourselves jammed against the glass, gaping straight down 200 feet at the tundra rushing by. False alarm. Just as suddenly, Erik heeled back to level. He gave us the grand tour, swooping through canyons, dodging over treetops, enjoying our queasy smiles. From what we could see of the river below, it was possible—no waterfalls, anyway—but obviously a handful. The clear, blue-green water swirled into brushy cutbanks and around boulders, raced through complex series of braids and rapids. The Redstone, by contrast, was a lazy tangle of serpentine loops winding across the tundra. We traced its course, then doubled back.

Fifty miles further on, at the head of the Ambler, was Natmaktugiaq Pass itself. We circled, studying the boulder-strewn river, the jagged 1,500-foot climb against a cliff wall, and the long portage toward the Noatak. Like the shadows below, doubts were creeping, but it was impossible to back down with honor. From the pilot seat, Erik grinned.

"If you don't make it, stop in on the way back to say hello," called Erik, as his freight canoe drifted downstream. He'd offered a lift to the mouth of the Redstone with his big outboard rig, and we'd accepted, intimidated enough by what we'd seen to figure we might need the time and energy further on. Peter and I exchanged glances. Fat chance we'd float back to Ambler with our tails between our legs. If it came to that, we'd duck up the Redstone and over Ivishak. In waking night-mares, I could see the entire population of Ambler, all 250, lined up at the landing, hooting as we slunk in.

We packed our gear, strapping it down into the plastic Old Town. The canoe wasn't much to look at, already patched and bat-tered, a broken thwart replaced with a slab of two-by-four, gouges showing the length of its green hide. But the Grateful Dead sticker on the bow, proclaiming *Blues for Allah,* was still in place. That, I told Peter, was the most important thing. A good canoe had to have a good name.

Good name or no, it didn't take long to discover that paddling the Ambler wasn't going to work. Thrashing madly, shoulders numb, we had to watch the bank to see if we were gaining or losing.

And so we grappled with the gentle art of lining. The idea is simple enough: you walk along the bank and drag your canoe with a rope. That was fine, except for a few minor details. You may have easy walking over gravel, but just as often it's a cutbank of rope-snarling, eye-gouging scrub willow. The choice is to curse through it a foot at a time or to ferry thirty or forty yards to the gravel bar on the inside bend—if there is one. Meanwhile, the cold rush of water shoves you into boulders and brushpiles. Another problem has to do with simple physics: if you hold the rope too tightly, *Blues for Allah,* like an idiot Saint Bernard, obediently follows you into the bank and grounds out. Too much slack and the current sweeps the bow out into a broach; if you're fool enough to hang on, the current reaches up like a big green hand, yanks the upstream gunwale down, and flips the whole boat over before you can pull in your breath. The Inupiat probably had all this figured out a few thousand years ago, but it was up to us, budding idiot-savants, to reinvent the technology.

So you need two ropes—one on the bow, one on the stern. You sling the bow rope across your shoulders, and into the hand away from the canoe. The stern rope goes to your near hand, arm outstretched behind you. With a little practice you can adjust the ropes by feel to maintain the right angle into the current, and after a few days you've developed the touch to weave along to the tune of screaming tendons.

There was one last detail. To make the whole thing work, we had to walk in the river, which was just a few degrees above ice. Otherwise there wasn't enough water under the keel, and we grounded out.

Numb, waterlogged toes begin to feel normal after a while, but Sears jogging shoes just weren't built to wear wet, and they started to disintegrate, with roughly 375 miles to the nearest store. Every morning I strapped them to my feet with silver duct tape; I'd forgotten my good boots on a gravel bar a month ago, a hundred miles up the Kobuk, and these seventeen-dollar wonders would have to last.

We fell into a steady rhythm, trading off between the glamorous post of scout, bear guard, and grayling snagger and the drudgery of muling 400 unruly pounds upstream. Six, eight, twelve miles a day, we slogged up past the Jade Mountains, toward the Cosmos Hills and into the rolling tundra of the Ambler lowland. Every mile or two, moose would erupt from the willows, singly or in pairs, belly-flopping off the bank or mowing swaths of brush flat in their bovine panic. There was no getting away from them; ecologically speaking, we were tramping through their notion of heaven. The ground was grooved by their trails and littered with piles of pelletized turds. Once we realized these clowns really didn't want a piece of us, their double-takes and antics were almost comic relief. But anything that stands six feet at the shoulder, weighs half a ton, and bulldozes wrist-thick alders is never just a sight gag.

Despite the moose and our fretting about bears, we spent most of our time looking down into the river. Tinted a surreal blue-green, it was so transparent that two feet of water seemed six inches instead, and we were constantly floundering into holes and dropoffs. The bottom was a shifting mosaic of gravel and sand, chunks of quartz crystal, jade pebbles, now and then a bone or an antler polished smooth by the current. At the end of a day, our pockets would be cluttered with rubble scrounged along the way. Then, each morning, we'd leave it all piled by the ashes of our campfire.

Keeping an eye on the river had a more practical angle. Arctic grayling hung against the cutbanks like sausages in a delicatessen counter. In that glass-clear water, though, they were far from easy marks. They'd dart after spinners without taking, and if a shadow fell across them, they were gone. But we usually picked up enough for a meal. Held in the light, the fish shimmered with the same blue-green iridescence as the river, as if it flowed within them, the tremendous dorsal fins a third as long as their bodies. We took five or six twice a day and gorged on them—grayling fried, grayling poached, grayling roasted in foil or sautéed in a gold pan with dried cheese. They became our staff of life, long after the novelty wore off. Twelve years later, I still like catching them, but I'd rather eat beans.

The miles fell behind, each bend a little victory, something new to look at. Climbing up a river has nothing in common with riding it downhill. I remember fixing my eye on a dark shape a half mile ahead, wondering if it would be a reclining bear, a stump, or a rock, and watching it slide closer as I leaned into the ropes. Only a rock this time. But what was that in the water up ahead, a beaver? In fifteen minutes I'd know. That protracted sense of unfolding left such imprints that, a year later, passing the same way, I could recognize a single dead tree or a boulder and remember the day we passed it.

We moved on. Five miles one day, eight the next, eleven, then four. Some bends were more stubborn than others, the corner seeming to recede as we fought through a chute or past a willow-clogged cutbank. But always the jumbled heave of the Schwatkas drew closer. We were skirting eastward along their southern flank, angling slightly toward them as we traversed the Ambler lowland. Ahead we could see the ridge that marked the river's abrupt northward sweep into the heart of the range. Tomorrow we'd be there.

The turn north was marked by a wide overflow area where the river spread out in a dozen channels cutting through a gray-white plain. A sunbleached wreckage of spruce logs collected here, stranded each spring by high water. We tried to imagine the scene at spring breakup: the river gushing from the valley mouth six vertical feet higher than now, standing waves tossing along entire trees like twigs. Here at the corner would be a huge mixing bowl, pans of overflow ice the size of parking lots grinding into motion, bulldozing new channels, wiping out entire islands. But now, in mid-July, the water was low and clear, the piles of logs and the expanse of naked gravel just a book to be read. Suddenly there was the percussive racket of a helicopter; it flashed over our heads and was gone. Third time today. Geological survey crews were mapping out the resources, preparing for the day when these hills would be worth money.

We made camp here, one of fifty-odd that summer. By this time the routine was as invariable as the chosen site: a dry, level bar of small gravel with driftwood handy, preferably an entire log jam. Peter set up the dome tent while I squatted at the water's edge cleaning fish. By the time I was done, a fire would be crackling along, and I'd cook as he stockpiled wood. A couple of times we tried switching jobs, but I'd end up complaining about fish scales in the rice and he'd shake his head at my choice of tent site. By that time of day, it was better to have firm expectations about what would come next, who would do it, and how. No gripes, no second guesses.

Fire, Food, dry Feet. The three Fs taken care of, we could relax. By then the sun would be dipping behind the hills and the air chilling—time to build the fire up, write in notebooks, pop the nightly ration of popcorn, drink the standard one cup of cocoa each, and one rationed sip of Yukon Jack from a plastic jug. Still hungry? Half a cold grayling for dessert. We were never that hungry. In the tent, Peter would meditate while I wrote. Snatches of the day would flicker past, and the last thing before sleep would be the sound of the river.

Into the Schwatkas. The valley was a narrowing funnel of rock forcing the river in on itself. Ahead, the brushy ridges merged into slate gray monoliths, 4,000 feet and rising. The river seldom slowed now, always tugging at our legs. We passed several homesteaders' cabins boarded tightly against bears, doors bristling with spikes like medieval castles. Boulders were common in the streambed now, and fishing fell off as pools grew less frequent. Looking back, we saw only mountains.

The river was narrowing fast—the current relentless, the water stinging cold. We would push forward a mile on good gravel, then bog down in ledges and boulders. Along one stretch white quartz slabs lay in the current like beluga whales. Further along was a recent plane wreck, a Cessna upended with prop bent and windshield shattered. No sign of the pilot. Maybe he'd been picked up by the chopper we'd seen.

Late in the afternoon we spotted something big in a pool above Ulaneak Creek. I cast a spinner, and instantly the rod doubled, a seven-pound arctic char leaping clear as line pressure turned him. Five minutes later I had another, and we decided to camp on the spot. As we feasted on the rich orange flesh, a lone caribou bull trotted past camp on some urgent errand. Mosquitoes were fierce for the first time in days, driving us into the tent even though a cool evening breeze fell down the valley. Apparently the last week of sunny weather had set off a fullblown hatch. With the worst ahead, it was a nasty portent.

By noon the next day, the Ambler had lost two more tributaries and become little more than a tumbling mountain stream. Progress dwindled to a crawl as both of us struggled thigh deep in the current, straining to ram *Blues for Allah* up one steep pitch after another. We almost lost it all in an instant as it snagged a rock and broached. Water gushed in and the bow line jerked from my hand. The canoe caught broadside, the weight of the river crushing in the gunwale, and then the plastic gave, slid free and swung into an eddy half-swamped.

There was no doubt now: we were in the Ambler canyons. Outcroppings and boulders hemmed us in and a huge rock face loomed ahead, summit drifted over by clouds. According to the map, there could be no more than five miles between us and the pass. The question was whether there would be enough water to get us there. Misfortunes seemed to be converging on us—no fish, rough going, wet sleeping bags, and clouds of mosquitoes descending like wolves on caribou. But all we had to imagine was Erik smirking sympathetically behind the counter as we recounted our woes. There was no way we were heading downstream now. Can't get worse, we told each other.

But those five miles took two long, wet, bug-spattered days. As we heaved up the creek one step at a time, hanging on to the canoe for balance and dear life, the headwall marking the pass grew before our eyes: 2,000 feet of gray cliff, furrowed, it seemed, into a monstrous frown. We knew we were past cabins and airplanes now; no one in his right mind would be traipsing around this vertical landscape. We were alone with the mountains from here to the Noatak.

The river gave out at about the same time we did. We stood at the foot of the pass, where the confluence of two unnamed tributaries had widened the canyon into a triangular basin maybe a half mile across. On three sides the Schwatkas swept up to 4,000 and 6,000 feet, gray towers a technical climber would appreciate.

The place was a miniature Shangri-la—dry tundra scattered with wildflowers, spruce clumps, and boulders arranged in the austere patterns of a Japanese ornamental garden. A waterfall gushed out of a canyon to the right, the rocks around the pool streaked with the brilliant blue and green of rich copper ore. A thought dark as a raven's wing floated past: one day this spot might be ripped to shreds by machinery, national park or no. The helicopter reminded me that an army of geologists was combing across the sweep of these mountains right now, waiting for the curves of supply and demand to meet at the required locus.

An odd piece of driftwood caught my eye as I stood by the pool, and it took shape in my hands, the curled horn of a Dall sheep ram. Its size and weight, ten annular growth rings barely readable, told a story—cold, storms, wolves. The ram had lived beyond our knowing and left its bones scattered down the canyon. I wanted to own it, this one small fragment of place, but it wasn't mine, and never would be. I turned away and tried not to look back.

We emptied the canoe and spread our gear over the gravel, sorting and repacking, preparing to carry what the river had carried. There would be three loads each, one light, one reasonable, one ridiculous. Rucksacks, fishing rods, and the rifle would be first; next, two packs containing food and camping gear; last, an ugly, bulging Duluth pack (genuine Boy Scout issue, overloaded by thirty pounds) and the canoe. We'd be lucky to find enough water to float it in fifteen miles. Until then it would be an eighteen-foot plastic albatross around our necks. I took a deep breath and looked up at Natmaktugiaq, "place to pack over." We were here, and it was time.

A beaten game trail wound through an open spruce grove and up the brushy slope into a new ecological sphere. Between us and the North Pole there were no more trees. I wondered if, in a good textbook's vegetation map, a line would run through the spot we stood on: the northern treeline. There was no sign whether the trees were gaining, losing, or just marking time. They looked thin but healthy enough, and then they just stopped. In this place of nearly perennial snow—there were dirty patches scattered in shadowed recesses even now, on July 20—a tree might need a couple hundred years to reach, say, ten inches in diameter. If you cut down enough to build a cabin here, it would take several lifetimes for replacements to grow, if they would at all.

The trail steepened into a claustrophobic alder maze. We zig-zagged back and forth, following the meandering instincts of moose and caribou, and finally abandoned the vanishing path in favor of a direct uphill assault. The brush thinned in a few hundred yards and was replaced by spongy alpine tundra, which in turn faded into a boulder field. The rim of the pass was just above.

We were breathing hard now, sweating in the afternoon haze and mobbed by a few thousand mosquitoes each. Every square inch of exposed skin was smeared with Vietnam-issue jungle juice, stuff that dissolves plastic buttons and burns like acid in your eyes. It kept the actual blood loss down to a level that didn't threaten death, but that wasn't the real problem. It was psychological warfare, airborne water torture. You felt the constant patter, and knew your back was crawling with living gray fur, hundreds of relentless snouts probing for a chink in your armor. A hand wiped down a sleeve would come away sticky, smeared with corpses, and you strained them through your teeth. Up your nose, in your eyes and ears, there was never a moment's rest. The blur of perpetual assault and the wail of wings brought on a creeping panic you had to ignore. They were simply a fact of existence, an elemental phenomenon like rain. You could ask, "is it bugging out today?" Yeah, a downpour. A bloody, bloodthirsty downpour.

We stood on the rim of the pass, panting. Ahead lay our corridor through the mountains, a half-mile wide stretch of rolling tundra framed by ragged limestone ridges and spires, half a mile above sea level. Fifteen hundred feet below, the Ambler wound off through the haze. The atmosphere was close, heavy with coming rain. We were in a race with the weather now. We needed everything up here before it broke; the trail was steep and slick enough without being greased by a downpour. There would be fewer rest breaks, a faster pace. It couldn't be helped.

Trotting down the mountain was child's play. You just keep your eyes on your footing, careful not to turn an ankle or step in the . . . bear shit. Fresh, soft, rank, gently steaming, right in the middle of the trail. No, it wasn't there when we went up. How big do you think . . . Should we climb back and get the gun? You do it. I'm going down. Let's make plenty of noise. Good idea. And so through the alders, thrashing and shouting, hoping to make sure we didn't catch a grizzly in a position where the only honorable action would be a charge. Knowing what I do now, I'm sure the bear in question was busy putting a few creeks between us and him. But the bear in our imaginations was lurking a bush away, drooling, a napkin tucked around its neck.

The canoe. Sisyphus would have understood the canoe. How the hell can you see with your head inside it, the thwart digging a groove in your shoulders as you crash uphill through the brush? All you can see is the ground before your feet and a dirty inverted bathtub full of bugs. Hands on the gunwales, fighting for balance, there's no way to swat or brush away the little vampires, and they know it. Places like eyebrows and earlobes, where repellent missed, are favored roosts. The only protection is your breath; you snort and puff at odd angles as if at stubborn birthday candles, and endure the sweat that dribbles rivulets of jungle juice into eyes and mouth. One thing for sure: even the most foul-tempered grizzly is going to burn rubber when he catches sight of this green, clumsy dragon staggering along, flinging curses to the sky. *Blues for Allah,* my ass.

The roar of blood in my ears nearly drowned out Peter's voice as I followed it up through the boulders. I could imagine the big Duluth with its Boy Scout suspension wrenching his shoulders at every step, gouging his spine, a hundred pounds of bad Karma. Each knowing the other was no better off kept our feet churning upward, and at last the grade eased, soft moss instead of shale before me. I heaved the canoe down and found myself back in the dazzling world of normal vision. Peter was flat on his back, wrestling with pack straps, sawing for breath. Mosquitoes clung like bats to the underside of his hat brim. His bloodshot eyes motioned toward the lowering sky; I looked up, and a raindrop splattered on my cheek.

The next three days collapsed into a haze of marshy tundra, rocky gullies, twisted ankles, and rain. Five miles north were two tiny lakes marking the Kobuk-Noatak divide, and we trudged back and forth, three ten-mile round trips, each one worse than the one before, culminating in a blind, tandem stumble with our heads jammed inside the canoe. Half sick with exhaustion, soaked to the skin, we spoke less and less and finally sank into a Neolithic stupor. I dimly recall squatting in the rain, eating peanut butter with my fingers and thinking in grunts, while Peter slept in a nearby puddle, his beard matted with dead mosquitoes and leaves. Lining up the Ambler was a fuzzy, fond memory, a time of order and comfort that seemed irrevocably lost. The Noatak, the next water we could expect to paddle, was still fifteen miles to the north.

We were hunkering in the tent when the storm hit. If we hadn't been, we might have laid down on the tundra and drowned like chickens. As it was, the wind almost took the tent, and the rain slammed in like buckshot. For most of a day we lay half-dazed, drifting in and out of dreams as our frail nylon envelope shuddered around us, folding double in the worst gusts.

I awoke to a hollow roar. The wind and rain had passed, and clouds scudded just over our heads, pouring off to the north. The mosquitoes were gone. Nushralatuk, the tiny creek leading to the Noatak, was rising by the minute, fed by runoff, and was deep enough to float the canoe. The rise wouldn't last for more than a couple of hours, but that would be enough. We'd been delivered by an Old Testament miracle. Still groggy, we pulled on wet clothes, threw in our gear, and shoved off.

Slamming off boulders, pounding over gravel, we barreled down the pass. Normally a trickle, the creek now rushed through a tight little canyon. *Blues for Allah* flexed and buckled around hairpin turns and flew down chutes, groaning and squealing as we flailed away, fighting for control. In the worst places we had to scramble in waist-deep icewater, wrestling down pitches too steep to run. We knew we were on the ragged edge, but we were far past caring. From the top of a rise we saw the Noatak River gleaming in the late sun.

We leaned into our paddles and flew down the Noatak, fleeing the pass as if it might rise up on its rocky haunches and give chase. With 300 miles ahead, we'd had enough. The country had kicked our ass, pure and simple, and all we wanted now was to get out before everything fell apart. Shoes, canoe, and ankles were patched with duct tape, but that wouldn't cover the deeper damage.

Peter and I weren't talking. Maybe we'd just spent too much time being wet and miserable together, or maybe it was because each of us had been broken, stripped of all dignity and pretense with his best friend watching. All I knew for sure is that we were ready to strangle each other. I sat in the stern of the canoe, grinding my teeth at small mannerisms, telling myself he was doing it to devil me: *Look, the bastard's about to stop paddling again to clean his glasses. There—what did I tell you?* Meanwhile, Peter was flashing me dark glares for equally heinous crimes.

To make matters worse, we'd miscalculated on food. We'd stuffed ourselves as we lined the Ambler, trying to lighten our load; now we were down to a couple pounds of macaroni, some salt, and a little stale peanut butter. It was fish or nothing. We gorged on grayling, trying to quiet bellies that cried for carbohydrates and fat. Later on, I'd hear Eskimos call it meat sickness. Even when we were full, we felt dizzy and hollow.

Stopping only to eat and sleep, we pushed downriver. Bands of caribou trotted past, hundreds crossing the Noatak, moving south. We eyed them for a while with atavistic lust, and finally decided to drop a small one, even if it wasn't exactly legal. My hunting experience back in Maine was limited to a few fiascos with deer, but when I yanked the trigger of the .35, a yearling bull flopped to the gravel. We hacked clumsy hunks off the hindquarters and dragged what was left into the brush. That night we ate wads of fat, rubbery fresh meat roasted on sticks, and life seemed good again.

On a gravel bar below the Cutler, we spotted a camp of floaters ahead—the first we'd seen in all our 500-odd miles so far. There were six of them sitting around the evening fire, and we pulled in, glad for some company. We could see at a glance that this was an outfit of high rollers—Kevlar canoes, flashy tents, and crisp matching GoreTex. Two of them were wearing Lord Mountbatten bush hats, the kind that snap up on one side. Compared to them, we looked like winos who'd just crawled out of a dumpster. "Howsitgoin?" A scattering of nods, but no one smiled, and no one asked us to sit down for a cup of tea, though a full bucket simmered on the fire. One of the younger men, more outgoing than the rest, shook hands, and we traded stories as the others exchanged sour looks.

They were on an expedition sponsored by some magazine and Ralston-Purina, canoeing across the Brooks Range by portaging between the Yukon, the Koyukuk, and the Noatak. This was serious business, and they didn't like sharing the river with anyone else— certainly not two grubby clowns in plastic ponchos and a junk canoe. When we offered that we'd come over the top from the headwaters of the Kobuk, the atmosphere around the fire got even chillier. We understood now. We were competition, Peary and Amundsen all over again. I craned my neck to peek at an open journal, and the phrase popped out: "When this ordeal fades into history . . ." Peter caught my eye, and I almost guffawed. These were genuine Arctic Heroes, better than we'd ever been. At that moment, the war between Peter and me was over, and we both stood there, grinning at each other, knowing.

Over the next few days, we seesawed back and forth, taking turns passing each other. The Heroes were on some sort of grim military schedule—on the river by nine, lunch at noon, off at five—while we traveled in the bright arctic night, when the wind was down, and camped at dawn. Every morning they'd paddle by our camp, and every evening we'd reel them in. We made sure each time to stop in on our way past, just to say hello, all relaxed and casual, just to stir them up. One red-bearded guy seemed especially infuriated by our ragtag presence; he muttered and chewed his lip until it almost bled. One day they covered thirty miles, and the next day we went forty before they caught up. Both sides could see where this was headed. The race was on for Kotzebue, over two hundred miles away.

After a brief council of war, we pushed off and paddled through the night, down past the Nimiuktuk and on to the Noatak Canyon, seventy miles with only two hour-long breaks. Compared to the pass, this was kid stuff, and with or without the Heroes, we were in a race. The caribou meat was turning rancid, and the macaroni was gone. We could buy a few supplies in Noatak village, fifty miles downstream. Eighty miles beyond that, Kotzebue floated like a mirage of epicurean delights—ice cream bars, chocolate, and beer shimmering ahead.

Down past the looming bluffs of the Canyon and into the maze of channels beyond the Kelly River, we moved in short punching strokes, riding the current, watching the miles swirl past in the pale midnight. Far overhead, the first wraiths of the aurora flickered, and the mountains seemed to answer, glowing purple, blue, and silver. Even *Blues for Allah* seemed alive, smooth and new again, singing through the water as if she knew what we saw and felt, and what we needed from her.

Of the 700 miles that summer, it's this last stretch I remember as best, probably because it was the one time we weren't out to prove anything—not to ourselves, to the country, or to anyone we met along the way. Somewhere in the arctic night, we passed the point of caring about anything but the quiet song of our going. The Arctic Heroes were forgotten somewhere behind us, faint echoes of what we'd once been. As we paddled along, small beneath the sky, the river carried us in her arms. All we were doing now was moving together, heading home to the sea.

*Westward I journeyed and landed on the shore
which is now Siberia. I followed the shore
towards the North. I saw some few people here,
but I was not interested so I kept on going. I
changed my course and tried for the inland and
found a number of deer [caribou]. I was very
much impressed with their pure way of living.
They did not seem to have any care as they
roamed everywhere. I was very interested and
decided to become one of them. Yes, I became a
deer. I shall never forget how many times I was
aroused from a light sleep by many intruders. So
many animals and human beings sought us.
Night and day we were on the alert; afraid,
afraid all the time. Even now I have a very deep
sympathy for them no matter where they are.
Their sleep is never heavy forgetful sleep.*

—from "Nathlook: Susie, My Name,"
in Lela Kiana Oman's *Eskimo Legends*

The River of Their Passing

▲▲▲▲▲▲▲▲▲

Willard Outwater leans into his binoculars, pointing across the Kobuk River toward a distant shimmer of movement. Everyone turns, suddenly attentive.

"Bulls?" asks Clarence Wood, shading his eyes. Willard relaxes and smiles. "Just small ones," he says. We lean back; there's a fresh pot of coffee, a crystalline August afternoon, and no hurry. Soon it will be time to eat. The aroma of caribou soup and roasting ribs wafts through camp.

"We just finish breakfast, all right, but *aarigaa* that fresh caribou meat," says one of the women. "That's what we come here for. The meat."

On the beach below the high bank, a half dozen carcasses lie on a bed of cut willows. One of the men works with an ax, lopping off antlers. Another cleans a rifle. Up in the two canvas wall tents, the elders rest while the women cook. Boys tend the fire, serve coffee, haul water. And always there is a lookout, scanning the north bank of the Kobuk, waiting.

It's caribou time at Onion Portage, twenty miles downstream from Ambler. The midnight sun of summer has faded, and the first frosts have burnished the tundra to shades of red and brown. Willow, birch, and balsam poplar blaze yellow—a last burst of color before the long white winter settles in. The air is so clear that distant mountains seem to be perfect miniatures you could reach out and touch with your hand. There might be more spectacular scenery, but none more haunting. Looking out over this land, you sense that this is a place where time does not exist. It has always been that way.

———

Through these mountains come the caribou in endless skeins, trotting down passes grooved with their trails, restlessly pushing toward their winter grounds south of the Brooks Range. This biannual migration to and from the calving grounds on the arctic coastal plain is something beyond mere spectacle; I still find myself overwhelmed by the passing of the caribou, at a loss to explain, even to myself, what I've witnessed.

The numbers alone are staggering. The western arctic herd is now the largest in Alaska, almost half a million animals. Their total range spans roughly 140,000 square miles, a roadless expanse stretching from Barrow in the north, east to the pipeline, south to Bettles and southwest to the Bering Sea coast—an area almost as big as Iowa, Illinois, and Michigan combined. Now at an all-time high, the western arctic is the largest caribou herd ever recorded in Alaska. Even so, it continues to increase at an annual rate of 12 percent, as it has for the past fifteen years. It's difficult to explain this phenomenal growth surge or to predict where it will stop, but then *Rangifer tarandus,* the barren ground caribou, has always been a creature of mystery. Along with the grizzly, Dall sheep, and musk-oxen, caribou survived the Pleistocene epoch and prospered where other species died out.

They are unlikely looking survivors at best. Barrel chested, low slung, spindly legged, with shaggy salt-and-pepper coats, bulging eyes, and enormous antlers, caribou seem more like a practical joke on the deer family than the incredibly tough, beautifully adapted creatures they are. Their thick bodies are powerful and designed to retain heat, and the stick-thin legs are tireless. Coats of multilayered hollow hairs are superb insulation as well as a built-in life preserver. Caribou can wade through six feet of snow on hooves like snowshoes, swim for miles, sleep comfortably at forty below zero, and prosper on a diet of frozen moss. The most impressive gift of all, though, is the caribou's ability to navigate unerringly over vast distances.

From June to August, the caribou of the western arctic herd roam north of the Brooks Range in loose bands of several to several hundred, wandering back and forth, feeding heavily on an abundance of grasses, willow, and succulent plants, building up weight for the winter. By September a prime bull will have two inches of fat on his rump, and weigh up to 350 pounds.

Larger groups form as the time for migration nears, and the herd begins to drift south. This is by no means a steady movement; a band may march fifty miles south, reverse their course the next day, and then swing to the west for no apparent reason. But finally, in response to cues known only to the caribou (the wind perhaps, or the amount of daylight, the angle of the sun, or a sudden snow) they surge southward. When they're moving in earnest, trotting together in long files, nothing can turn them; they plunge through rivers, clamber over mountains, and seem to almost ignore the dozens of Eskimo hunters waiting at crossings to make their fall harvest.

There is no exact timetable, no certain route. Some years the migration is brisk and purposeful, with most of the herd crossing the Kobuk River between the villages of Ambler and Kiana during September. In other years, the movement may be sporadic and last well into November. A valley overflowing with caribou one season may be nearly silent the next.

Two Octobers ago, a huge band—ten, maybe even twenty thousand—milled around behind Ambler for two weeks, trapped on the north bank of the Kobuk by flowing ice just before freeze-up. No one could remember so many so close to town. They bulldozed trails through the willows within sight of the school, plowed up the tundra, and a few confused animals trotted into town as if to visit, sending the hundreds of chained sled dogs into a frenzy. Pilots had to buzz strays off the runway before they could land, and kids made a game out of hiding by trails and counting how many animals they touched. Village men shot dozens, perhaps hundreds, and filled their meat caches to overflowing (the subsistence limit is five animals per hunter per day), but the caribou kept coming. The next year, caribou were relatively scarce near Ambler; many crossed the Kobuk near the Squirrel River, seventy miles to the west.

Caribou may travel 300 to 500 miles on one of their marches. Biologists have fitted animals with satellite tracking collars that precisely record movements, in an attempt to understand where caribou travel, and why. One pattern that emerges is that an individual will almost certainly return to the calving ground where it was born. Fidelity to a calving ground is, in fact, how biologists have finally determined the boundaries of the dozen herds in Alaska, and debunked the theory that there is only one huge herd made of single animals who move randomly and change allegiances on a whim. State biologist Jim Dau says, "No matter how far caribou wander, they almost always sort themselves out and return to their own calving grounds. It's pretty amazing how they do that."

This homing mechanism is almost certainly a learned response, some sort of imprinting on an area, but instinct could also play a part. Sensitivity to magnetic fields, the sun, or sense of smell may help in the actual navigation. *Why* they do it is another question. There must be a reason why the western arctic herd returns to the Utukok Hills each June to have their young. Calving grounds are generally areas with low concentrations of predators and, at least as important, parasitic insects, notably warble flies and mosquitoes. (Caribou spend much of their summer avoiding the swarms of insects that plague them; a single warble fly is enough to stampede a herd, and there is little doubt that severe infestations of warble fly larvae, burrowed beneath the hide, are a real threat to survival.)

This loyalty to calving area raises questions about oil and mineral development on the arctic coastal plain. Most biologists agree that disturbance of the calving grounds will drive caribou to less favorable places, which will lead to diminished survival of young, and, ultimately, fewer animals. While the struggle over oil exploration in the Arctic National Wildlife Refuge (the calving grounds of the Porcupine River herd) has grabbed the most media attention, the western arctic herd's calving grounds may be just as threatened by the enormous coal deposits east of Point Lay, said to contain up to *one tenth* of the world's supply. Pregnant cows generally refuse to give birth near any human disturbance, in contrast to summering bulls, who graze along the pipeline and among North Slope oil rigs, much to the delight of EXXON and ARCO publicity directors.

Calving grounds are not the only critical areas in a herd's range. By their very nature, caribou require huge expanses of pure wilderness, and any sort of human development poses a threat to their unrestricted movement. Roads are especially likely to deflect migration, though to what extent remains uncertain. What *is* certain is that caribou and civilization are inevitably converging, and careful decisions must be made over the next two decades to ensure that caribou will roam Alaska a century from now.

The importance of caribou is far more than a matter of aesthetics. The fortunes of many species are tied directly to the condition of the herd. "Think of a complex wheel with spokes that run in multiple directions," says Dau. "Caribou are at the hub." Wolves, grizzlies, foxes, wolverines, and ravens all depend on caribou for food; moose and sheep are preyed upon more heavily when caribou numbers are low. Grazing and trampling affect most tundra plants, and even the land is shaped, marked by thousands of miles of beaten trails. Quite simply, without caribou the arctic ecosystem would not be itself.

The people of the northwest arctic depend on caribou as they always have. The ancient bond between caribou and humans is witnessed by artifacts and bone fragments dating back ten thousand years. Dozens of Eskimo hunters like Willard Outwater and Clarence Wood still travel to Onion Portage, one of the old meeting places, to gather the land's gifts. Some families travel up to 200 miles in open boats—skiffs, in some cases—to be here for this momentary flood of abundance. There was a time when the hunters speared animals from kayaks, set snares of thong, or drove bands into natural culs-de-sac where they were taken with bow and arrow. Every scrap was utilized— skins for clothing and tents, bones and antler for tools, stomach contents for greens—but that time is past, seventy years and more.

Still, this is more like gathering than hunting, as it's understood in the Lower 48. A premium is placed on fat rather than horn size, and most animals are shot in the river at point-blank range, several at a time, and towed to shore for butchering. Meat is the object, but there is more: hunting caribou, more than any other single act, defines the Inupiat to themselves. Men nod with satisfaction as they shoot into a band of fat bulls and see them drop; women laugh and smile, red to the elbows as they wield their razor sharp, wedge-shaped *ulus,* rejoicing in abundance. The hunt ends when the boats are full, wallowing with carcasses. If the caribou are early or late, or cross somewhere else, the hunters may stay a week and go home emptyhanded. The land gives freely, or inexplicably withholds its riches.

In the end, no amount of description, no volume of words can fully explain caribou. They are enigmatic creatures who seem to offer little in the way of spiritual connection to humans. Even the Inupiat have largely forgotten the small ceremonies of reverence their fathers knew, forgotten the time, just a century ago, when the caribou disap- peared from most of the region, and The People sometimes starved. We *naluaqmiut* are much further removed; we don't easily see ourselves in these beasts, as we do in wolves or whales. Their bovine, bulging eyes ask for nothing. Their intelligence and spirit violate our preconceptions and seem, at best, indifferent to our understanding. We're forced to retreat into facts and words, to objectify in our attempt to know them. "A lot of people don't hold caribou in very high regard," observes Jim Dau. "They think of them as a pot of soup or as so many inches of fat, or a number of points on antlers. But they are truly remarkable creatures, remarkable as any wolf or bear, if not more so." What is most remarkable about caribou, I think, is that which eludes us: their spirit, the pure, uncompromising force that drives them across the land.

I think back to one September day four years ago. I'd made camp where the confluence of the Hunt and Nuna rivers forms a funnel for caribou, a few miles west of Onion Portage. The roughly triangular field there has been a pathway for generations; some of the trails are a foot deep, and bleached antlers lie scattered across the tundra. I'd traveled fifty miles from Ambler in my jetboat to escape the seasonal commotion along the Kobuk—boats roaring back and forth, camps at every bend, volleys of gunfire. I had my rifle with me, but hunting was only a pretense, an excuse to offer my Eskimo friends if they asked. I'd come for something else—just to watch, to see. Here there was only the voice of the land, wind, and water and the hush of huge empty space. I'd been sitting for two days, staring out across the tundra, slowly emptying myself of thoughts, waiting at this place as men must have always done.

I was on the morning's fourth cup of coffee when the alders on the slope a mile off began to move. It might have been the wind, but the motion was too great, too sudden. I adjusted my binoculars, and bushes became caribou—dozens, then hundreds streaming toward me. I dashed to the blind I'd made at the center of the field and waited, pulse thundering in my ears, as they came. At first there was only a mass of shapes, but then the white manes and antlers of the herd bulls shone in the low sun, and I could pick out calves skittering along the fringes of the onrushing mob. I became aware of a low, steady commotion: grunts between mothers and calves, click of antlers and leg tendons like a thousand castanets, and, beneath it all, the muffled thud of hooves. Strung out in a long file ten abreast, they poured down the hill, more than a thousand now. Crouched behind my flimsy wall of brush and burlap, the leaders nearly upon me, I fought back the urge to run.

Twenty yards away, a cow sensed me. She froze, staring, and her alarm rippled back through the herd until the front ranks had all come to a halt. They stood stiff legged and silent, regarding this strange-smelling thing that blocked their way. Then, without an outward sign, they reached a consensus and began to move again. The herd surged forward, parted to include me, and I became an island in the river of their passing. I had meant to count—as a way of explaining to myself and others what I'd seen—but numbers were suddenly meaningless, impossible. Through the morning and into the late afternoon the caribou flowed by. Now and then one would give a start and roll its eyes, but most simply glanced my way and trotted past, intent on their timeless, urgent business to the south.

Then, as suddenly as they had come, they were gone. The tundra before me was as empty as if they had never been. For a time I had been included in the mystery; it had moved about me, and silently accepted my presence. Now only the barnyard scent and the pummeled earth remained to show this had not been a dream, a great passage of ghosts. I sat in the dusk, waiting, but the land was silent.

The kemich *[inviting hosts] are not satisfied because their best runner did not win the race. They want to pick up a few runners and make them run again to show who is the best runner. Lots of argument right there!*

They pick out older people—middle-aged— from the visitors and the village for racing. And now the visitor runners win the race again. People are satisfied right there. Trouble is over. Village boss, he is satisfied the village runner gets half the race anyhow. Just about even!

. . . Racing business is over, eating business is over. Now they start different kinds of games. They start to jump. So they kick five or six feet up and kick a ball. One time one Kobuker kicks the window above that ball. The kemich *win that kicking business. After that visitor women tell them, 'Us women are going to kick too—see us win!' And two young Kobuk women win again—kick higher than the rest of them.*

> —from the narrative of Oolyak (Stonewall Jackson), in Louis Giddings' *Kobuk River People*

Beat the Qaaviks

⌃⌃⌃⌃⌃⌃⌃⌃⌃

The Noatak Lynx are playing their archrivals from the coast, the Kivalina Qaaviks (Wolverines). The green-clad Lynx are up by seven points late in the fourth quarter, but the Qaaviks, like their namesake, are going down fighting. The Noatak middle school students, thirty strong, chant and clap in deafening unison with the three cheerleaders:

"BEAT 'EM, BUST 'EM, THAT'S OUR CUSTOM . . ."

From the coaches' seat on the Noatak bench I hold up two fingers, and the Lynx set up a half court offense, passing, feinting, using the clock as we've practiced a dozen times. But Steven Koenig, the Qaavik star forward, anticipates a pass and steps up for the steal. He drives the length of the court and swoops past a defender, flipping in a reverse layup and collecting a foul. A roar of dissent goes up from the partisan crowd, while the thirty Kivalina fans, windburned and frostbitten after their sixty-mile snow machine ride, shout their approval.

"He sure foul!"

"Man, ref, so cheap!"

"Just like you can't see!"

"Don't listen to them, they don't know nothing!"

The two local officials, one a white high school teacher, the other a young village man, a former Lynx, try to ignore the abuse. After he's ridiculed by name, though, the young man turns to the offender and offers his whistle and shirt.

"Want to ref, *kumaq?*" Kumaq is Inupiaq for head louse. The older women, bundled in their bright flowered calico parkas even in the gym heat, cackle; others join in the laughter, and the game goes on.

Koenig, whose father captains a traditional whaling crew, sinks the free throw, and the lead is down to five. Rattled, my sophomore point guard dribbles the ball off his foot as he tries to break Kivalina's press. Koenig has his radar switched on now; he sinks an impossible eighteen-foot jumper off the inbound pass, and the Lynx lead by two with thirty seconds on the clock. I call time, and my team gathers in a tight huddle as an earsplitting female voice launches into a singing call and response, a third of the crowd, child and adult alike, joining in. The heating ducts rattle and the walls of the tiny gym boom with a hundred screaming voices:

"Beat the Qaaviks . . ."

"BEAT THE QAAVIKS . . ."

"Somebody oughta . . ."

"SOMEBODY OUGHTA . . ."

"Somebody gonna . . ."

"SOMEBODY GONNA . . ."

"Beat 'em . . ."

"BEAT 'EM . . ."

The Lynx inbound the ball, beat the press, and manage to ice the ball for the win. Kids pile out of the stands, mobbing the home team, high-fiving and joining in a hand-linked jumping mass at center court. Parents beam their satisfaction, and old men hobble up to me, showing the gaps in their teeth.

"We sure win them, ah?"

"Real good our boys this time!"

"Sure glad we never lose to them Kivalinas!"

I shake hands and smile back, equally relieved. The Lynx are in the chase for the regional championship, and everyone expects great things of us. After four years of coaching, I know how much winning means to the village, and how quickly I'll be blamed if we lose.

The crowd disperses slowly. Tomorrow is the second game, and then, weather permitting (Kivalina is notorious for the worst winds in the region), the Qaaviks will fly in chartered Cessna 207s back to their home village; the Noatak girls, who have been playing there, will return on the backhaul. The total cost for transportation is over $400, and this is an inexpensive weekend, since the two villages are relatively close to each other and to Kotzebue, the home base of the charter company. When you figure that there are eight small villages in the Northwest Arctic Borough School District with basketball teams, and that each school plays between ten and twenty regular season games, two per trip, you get an idea of the expense—and that's just travel. Not counting the buildings, the yearly cost for the school district's basketball program—coaches, uniforms, equipment, travel—is well over a hundred thousand dollars. The People want basketball that badly. The residents of Ambler, when asked for input on the design of their new school, specified that a gym was first on the list, and they got what they asked for: a basketball floor with cramped classrooms tacked on as an apparent afterthought.

The whole phenomenon is astounding when you consider that fifteen years ago, only three of the ten villages in the NANA (Northwest Arctic Native Association) region had gymnasiums; twenty years ago, only Kotzebue, the hub of the region, had one. Noatak has had its gym for less than ten years. Each village was guaranteed its own high school (and by extension, its own basketball court) by the state supreme court decision known as the Molly Hootch consent decree, which was implemented in the mid-1970s. The suit argued that every child had a right to a complete education in the home village, instead of being sent to large regional schools. The state of Alaska was obliged to build a high school in each village that requested one—close to a hundred buildings, and the teachers to staff them.

Luckily for the state, implementation of the Hootch decree coincided almost exactly with the completion of the oil pipeline. In Noatak, the last village in the region to get their school (completed in fall of 1981), construction costs ran well over a million dollars, and the tab for a new elementary was nearly two million.

Apart from education, the state's lavish expenditure altered village life forever. Noatak is a typical case: in just a few years the new gym with its basketball court has become the center for the young of the village, just as the church is for the elders. Many students arrive at school a half hour early so they can shoot baskets, and they'd play ball every day in physical education class if they could hound me into it. After school there is an hour and a half of basketball practice. All but two of fifteen high school boys are on the Lynx team, and the percentage is nearly as high for the girls on the—dare I say it—Lynkettes. After practice the kids walk home, eat supper, do some chores or a little homework, and head back for their scheduled hour in the gym, which they get six nights a week. While they're waiting for the elementary school and junior high students to have their turn (toddlers are out there dribbling rubber play balls, seven-year-olds heaving shots over and over at the hopelessly high rims), they socialize and do homework. At precisely 8:00 P.M. they're on the floor, shooting around and choosing sides. After their time is up, they watch the young men of the village play city league pickup games. There's a ten o'clock weeknight curfew for students; at the constable's siren they head home to watch television or finish their homework. At 7:30 the next morning, a handful of the faithful are out there again, shooting layups.

You won't find many tall players this far north; pureblooded Inupiat reach six feet only rarely, while the largest half-breeds clear six two. The big man for most teams is around this height, while occasionally a true monster of six four might emerge, forcing coaches to devise defensive strategies to neutralize this Eskimo Abdul-Jabbar. Lack of height prevents most otherwise talented players from ever going on to college ball, where the average guard is taller than most village centers. If the local sport of choice were hockey or baseball, the ranks of college and even professional teams might well be sprinkled with wiry, explosive defensemen and shortstops with names like Ontogook, Foxglove, and Cleveland.

But basketball is one of the few sports that could have caught on in the Alaskan bush. Field sports are out of the question; in the northwest arctic, the first snow flies in September, and is still melting when school lets out. It's too cold outside for hockey most of the year.

Individual sports—cross-country running, skiing, and wrestling—would seem perfect for small schools, since they require little equipment or indoor space, and even schools like Deering, with its nine high school students, could field athletes on an equal basis. A few years back, cross-country skiing was a varsity sport in the northwest arctic; Noatak, in fact, produced some of the finest skiers in the district, until basketball came along. Now skiing is officially dead as an interscholastic sport. Wrestling and cross-country running have yet to gain regional acceptance, though in 1982, Eliot Sampson, a pureblooded Inupiat from Noorvik, shattered the course record on his way to winning the state cross-country title. Eliot, nicknamed "caribou legs" in his home village, ran away from everybody—the big-school Alaskan urban kids with their high-tech shoes and expert coaches—smiled shyly, and returned home to lead Noorvik to the state finals in basketball.

When you see how the northwest arctic villages have dominated the state in basketball, you can better understand the lack of interest in other sports. The best local teams, some from schools with fewer than thirty students, sometimes beat schools six or eight times larger—Kotzebue, Nome, and Dillingham. Since the 1983-84 season, there has been a new division of the state championships, specifically for schools of under fifty students. Since then, northwest arctic teams have won eight state titles and finished second several times. The statistic is more impressive when you consider the competition. Every year there is at least one team in the finals with Caucasian players five inches taller and twenty-five pounds heavier than their Eskimo opponents. In1985, for example, my Noatak boys' team, with our tallest player at five feet ten inches, faced Klawock, which had two players at six feet four—and almost won. In other years, Kiana, Ambler, and Noorvik have won the title against far larger opponents.

There are different ways of interpreting the impact of all this time spent at the gym. Even though parents turn out for all the games, many also complain that basketball takes up too much of their children's lives. Few boys are out hunting ptarmigan or rabbits after school, or following their fathers on their traplines. Most girls have never learned the traditional skills of cutting fish or preparing caribou sinew for thread, though their mothers do these things and much more in everyday life. A common complaint among parents is, "*Adii,* just like my kids are never home. Always school."

Much of that school time is pure basketball. Parents could certainly stop or slow this trend if they wished, but exerting such control seems a strange notion to most Inupiat; children have always been free to choose. Besides, school is recognized as a good thing, as it has been since the first missionaries established schools around the turn of the century, drawing scattered camps together into villages. From that time on, the Inupiat were moving inexorably toward a future of orange balls and fast breaks, toward a time when the warm, communal atmosphere of the gym would seem a natural extension of their culture.

Clarence Wood takes a darker view. Though his two boys have

both played ball for the Ambler Grizzlies, he's never seen a game. Even the year that the boys won a state title, he refused to watch. "I tell you what," he grumbles, pointing at the gym across from his house. "That's a bullshit in there. One big bullshit." Disgusted, he loads his sled to go caribou hunting alone.

Basketball is more than a childish preoccupation. There are no less than six men's city league teams in Noatak, each with a roster of at least eight, plus three women's teams. Nearly everybody between ages 18 and 35 plays on one of these; there are two hours per weeknight allotted to city league, and on weekends when the gym is free of school-sponsored games or activities, the games start at six and go to eleven, sometimes on both Friday and Saturday nights: the Renegades versus the Bullets, the Napaaqtugmiut against the Warriors, the Cousins versus the Women's City League, and so on. No one remembers the scores, and few remember who won from week to week, though some games are hotly contested, sometimes degenerating into shouted obscenities and shoving matches. Players jump from one roster to another, and the style of play is freewheeling, more reminiscent of in-your-face street ball than the organized play of the high school teams.

Perhaps the saddest vision in village basketball is that of a former high school hero, a former regional all-star, who now lives to play city league. Maybe he was a great high school athlete, but he was also only five feet seven inches, and had no desire to leave the village for college in the first place. He stayed in school mostly for basketball, kept up his grades so he could travel with the team. Now, five years after graduation, he is still living at home, sleeping most of the day, waiting for the gym to open at 10:00 P.M. so he can relive a time when people cheered him and the games mattered. There are more of these city league heroes than you'd wish. Some actually consider themselves professionals because local sponsors buy them uniforms and fly them to tournaments. One former player of mine smiled as he described city league as his "career." Some go away to college or technical school and come back six months later; a few enlist in the Army. I can't help wondering what their lives would have become without basketball—better, worse, or the same?

You could consider all this basketball a travesty, Outside influence run amok, all these thousands of man-hours wasted. True, many of the young have become much less active in traditional ways, but others do run traplines and hunt caribou and keep their extended families in firewood in addition to playing ball; food does get cooked, new mukluks are sewn, and babies are raised. Many villagers will say there is less drinking because of the gym, and certainly most of the young men in town and many of the women are in fine shape from their nights of running up and down the floor. Serious violence—fights and gunplay—seem to be on a decline regionwide, and maybe this decrease is partly due to a healthy release of aggression on the court.

Also, basketball, especially at the high school level, is a tremendous source of village pride. When Kiana swept to both the boys' and girls' state titles in 1984, the village and the region exploded in a frenzy of Eskimo patriotism. In a time when the Inupiat find themselves increasingly dominated by outside forces, basketball is, paradoxically, a source of assurance and identity.

Basketball also provides a community focus, taking over the function of traditional Eskimo games. In the past, a community would divide into teams or a neighboring village would visit for the purpose of friendly competition, and there would be an evening or even days of games, resembling a modern track and field meet in organization and aspect. The individual events were, for the most part, ones that could be held in the more limited space afforded by a community building or even a large home during the long, dark winter. Feasting, exchanging of gifts, trading, wooing, and simple socializing were as important as the actual competition. Some games focused on brute strength. Consider the head pull, a woman's game where two competitors faced off in pushup position with a wide strap or belt hooked over their necks. The idea was to pull the opponent over a line or yank the belt free of her arched neck. Other games, like the one-foot-high kick, were a test of both agility and explosive power; here, a small hide ball was suspended on a string, and the competitor had to take off from one foot, strike the ball with the other foot, and then land balanced on the striking foot. The event was held like a modern high jump, with competitors eliminated as they missed, the mark growing higher until only one remained.

Some events, like the seal hop and the ear pull, were simple tests of pain and endurance. In the seal hop, contestants were in a lowered pushup position on toes and knuckles; the idea was to hop the longest distance without allowing any other part of the body to touch the ground. The hopping surface was often hard or irregular, and skin, even flesh, was abraded from the knuckles as the contestants hopped along the floor, muscles straining.

There were other games: the two-footed high kick, leg wrestling, finger pull, and stick jump. People still play these games, but less and less frequently at the village level.

It's basketball they want. On winter nights the cry echoes across the expanse of bush Alaska:

BEAT 'EM, BUST 'EM . . .

In just a few years, it's become their custom.

*The mountains between Kobuk and Noatak
became my home. For a few years I lived as a
wolf among a large pack of wolves. We would
travel all over, and way up north and back
to these mountains. Among these high
mountains I became myself again. Somewhere in
the midst of the forest I left my garb quite
lifeless. That is the only meaning I can give it.
My carcass was just a discarded garment that no
longer was needed. I had no feeling or pity
for it. Never to be worn again or never to see
again, I left it there. I had no interest in what
should happen to it.*

— from "Nathlook: Susie, My Name,"
in Lela Kiana Oman's *Eskimo Legends*

Running with the Wolves

▲▲▲▲▲▲▲▲▲

Everything about Clarence Wood is understated, everything except his eyes—deepset slits, impassive and penetrating. The angular face is dark and weatherbeaten, bearing the purple-black scars of repeated frostbite. Grizzled, close-cropped hair and moustache match the face as the face matches the body—lean, compact. When he speaks, Marlboro dangling, his full lips hardly move, and his voice is breathy and low. But there is that lupine glint to his eyes that I find unsettling, though I've known him for twelve years and call him friend.

Twenty-five years ago, working with a sled dog team or on snowshoes, Clarence was a tough, resourceful hunter, able to stay out for days and weeks on end with a light pack, ignoring cold and hardship that would have killed many men. Now, astride a metal dog that can hit 70 miles an hour, he is the ultimate predator, the apotheosis of Eskimo hunting technology. Distances that once took days now take hours, and mobility translates into power. When Clarence spots an animal, the old ways, the patient, meticulous ways, are suddenly no longer relevant.

"If you find a trail that look fresh, you put your hand down and feel it. If it's real hard, maybe from last night. A little hard, maybe this morning. Real soft, that means right now. Drop your sled and just go get him."

A typical understatement. In this harsh, remote landscape, the hunt is seldom a foregone conclusion. A wolverine or a wolf covers a huge stretch of territory in a short time and usually rough country at that—mountain slopes, willow-choked creekbeds, dense timber where the snow lies six feet deep. It takes years of experience just to move over this terrain without getting stuck. Or lost. Or worse. The wolves, too, usually hear a hunter coming from miles away and know enough to disappear into places a machine can't follow.

"Smart, those buggers. Smart as a man. Start this way, go that way, disappear like nothing."

In the darkness of a November morning, it's 30 below zero. Clarence is in his yard across from the Ambler school, packing his sled. I stop to talk, putting off my preparations for class.

"Where you headed today, Clarence?"

"Guess I'll go through Ivishak." He ties a gas can into his sled, snaps a loaded clip into his carbine. "Go home and pack your sled. Should be pretty nice." Though we've often traveled together, we both understand today's invitation is a joke.

"I have to teach your kids," I reply, and he shrugs.

"Good luck, Clarence."

"Thank you."

He heads north, riding hard, two hours at full speed up the Redstone valley, then up over Ivishak Pass into the Cutler, part of the Noatak drainage. It's a route the Kobuk Eskimos have used for centuries. But Clarence covers the sixty-odd miles in a time his forefathers could not have imagined. At the crest of the pass he breaks west and rides a trail marked only in his mind, cutting from one mountain creek to another, through brushy bottomland and along hillsides so steep that he sometimes has to stand with both feet on the uphill running board, leaning all his weight into the slope. Looking, always looking, for that telltale flicker of movement in a still white landscape or for the etched line of a fresh trail, he barrels along, self-contained in his true element, a hundred miles from anyone.

Clarence has crossed many sets of tracks today, most hardly worth a glance: the catlike, precise line of red fox; the day-old signature of several wolves; caribou. He pauses on an open knoll for a cigarette and coffee from a steel thermos. After four hours of the machine's clatter, the silence has its own roar, punctuated by the sharp pings of his cooling engine. Clarence, half deaf from decades of motors and gunshots, hears little past his own breathing. Although he's seen nothing, he's not discouraged. If not today, then tomorrow or the next day. It's time to work homeward. Too cold for man or machine to linger—forty below and falling, as the brief daylight fades.

Twenty miles from home, he sees the tracks. Here something has crossed his incoming trail. He swings around for a closer look: the distinctive two-and-two pattern of a running wolverine, crisp, yet feather-soft to the touch. The wolfish glint in his eyes sharpens. Moving quickly, with a precision born of repetition, he prepares for the chase. The hardwood basket sled, with its toolbag, gas can, ax, and tarp, is unhitched, and he checks his rifle, a military-looking carbine called a Ruger Mini-14. Made of stainless steel, it has a wide-angle scope and fires twenty rounds of .223 as fast you can pull the trigger. He lays the gun on the snowmobile seat and straddles it, stock forward, ready for a quick shot. Then he's off, racing both the wolverine and the coming darkness—down into a creek bed for several miles, then up a steep slope and along a ridge, five hundred feet above the valley floor.

On the downslope Clarence catches up. A quarter mile ahead, a dark shape lopes through the brush. His thumb jams the throttle wide open, and the machine leaps forward in a cloud of snow. The wolverine, with its strange bounding gait, can't hope to outrun its pursuer. But it has intelligence and incredible toughness, plus an ability to go where the machine can't. It dodges into a thick willow clump and up a gully, running hard for a sheer rock face several hundred yards away. Clarence angles to cut off the escape. He slams through the brush, rifle clamped under one leg. The chest-high willows, brittle with cold, shatter into a spray of sticks.

The gap is closing—two hundred yards, one hundred. He vaults a hard drift and flies twenty feet, smashes down on one ski, leans back. The wolverine puts on a burst of speed and reaches the slope. Clarence swerves into a braking skid, swinging up his carbine in one motion. The first shot is off before the machine halts, high and to the left. The scope's crosshairs waver with each heartbeat. Five more rounds bracket but miss the animal, now far above in the rocks. But then it pauses to look back before going over the crest. Clarence fires again and the wolverine tumbles, snarling.

He examines his prize, a prime forty-pound male with a thick, coffee-tone pelt. It's his second of the season, for fifteen days of hunting. He nods to himself, almost smiles. Properly cared for, the skin will bring as much as $400 from a village seamstress, maybe $100 less if he sends it to a buyer in Seattle. Most wolf and wolverine pelts are used locally, prized for parka ruffs that shed frost and outlast anything else.

Now that the concentrated whirl of the chase is past, Clarence notices that the tip of his nose and one cheek are frozen hard. He thaws them with his hand until he feels the scorching tingle of waking nerves. Just another scar. But there's a cracked ski and a snapped spring on the Cat. There goes $70 off the top, plus downtime for repairs. Always something: a burned drive belt, a torn track, a seized bearing. The available machines—Arctic Cat, Ski Doo, Yamaha, Polaris—are built for the Lower 48 recreational market, not for day-in, day-out pounding and pulling in the arctic. At forty below, oil thickens to paste, gas loses volatility, and steel can snap like plastic.

Hunters carry spare parts, even entire spare engines in their sleds and often improvise repairs far out in the country. There's the story of an Anaktuvuk man who, confronted with a disintegrated rear axle assembly, carved new parts out of wood. Clarence once fashioned handlebars out of two pairs of locking pliers and limped home a hundred miles, working the throttle with his knee.

Of course, real breakdowns—the ones you can't fix in the field— are a fact of life, especially for the hunter who believes in one speed for long hauls. Even a new machine can take just so much of what Clarence calls "full blast," especially while lugging a full sled through soft snow. Usually a hunter tells someone where and when to start searching, but there's no telling where a wolf might go, and how the weather might turn. When storms sweep away the trail, a stalled machine becomes just another snowdrift. More than once Clarence has spent days wrapped in a sled tarp waiting for a blizzard to pass or for rescuers to arrive, but even now, at age fifty-five, he shrugs and says, "Well, I hate to break down, all right," then heads out alone at forty below.

It doesn't take an accountant to figure out that this mechanized fur hunting is often no more than a marginal business. One day—one without complications—will cost between $25 and $50. A good (and lucky) hunter might average two weeks per wolf or wolverine, with a few foxes thrown in. A very successful four-month season might be seven wolves, four wolverines and twenty foxes, together worth about $7,000. Only a few hunters do that well. On the other hand, major repairs can run $1,000 or more, and a new machine, which might last three seasons, costs up to $6,000.

In the summers, Clarence finds work in construction away from the village, and his wife makes birchbark baskets and travels back and forth to Kotzebue, where she has a job at the hotel. Their cash income is barely enough to provide for an extended family and to pay for gas and parts. Year-round jobs—even if they were available in their home village—are unacceptable from a spiritual standpoint. Unlike some Eskimos who have come to regard a job in the cash economy as an end in itself, Clarence and others like him see such jobs as a means only: a means to live up to the values of their fathers, who knew that a successful man, a real man, was a skilled hunter. And Clarence's family and relatives (seemingly a quarter of the village) depend on the meat he provides—caribou, moose, beaver, or bear—at every meal. Quite simply, these people would be impoverished without the land's gifts.

Yet at times I rest uneasy, haunted by the spirits of running wolves, unsure what to make of this latest permutation of Inupiat culture. The aesthetics of chasing down animals with machines doesn't concern Clarence, and I wish it did; but he didn't invent the machines nor our concepts of fair chase and conservation. If I broached the subject he'd consider me a fool. The new technology is just another means toward an ancient end. Eskimos have embraced snowmobiles and semiautomatic rifles so that the seams between cultures are scarcely visible.

Still, something seems lost or gone awry; maybe it's not the wolves at all, but that I'd like to believe there is still a place in the world where a fur-clad figure waits patiently with a spear, humming spirit songs rather than cursing at pistons. There is assurance in that vision; perhaps it would serve as a landmark to guide us home, or at least to mark our trail. But I have no right to expect Clarence to be a living museum while I teach his children to use computers and speak standard English. I have to let my abstract notions go, along with my inclination to judge.

For untold generations, the Kobuk Eskimos lived in balance with their world, and often they, not the animals they hunted, were the endangered species. If the land offered something, it was unquestioningly, thankfully accepted as a gift from a limitless storehouse, something that allowed The People to live. As long as they showed proper reverence by such rituals as slitting the dead animal's trachea—*nigiluq*—the animal spirit would escape and be reborn, to be hunted again. There was no burden of souls.

Clarence still practices *nigiluq*—believes, too, in the perpetual abundance it implies. Once after he'd returned from a spring hunt I asked him if he'd seen many caribou on the flats. With a rare, expansive smile he replied, "Lots. You could never finish 'em." Lllotttsss. He said the word as if it had ten letters, lips drawn back to bare tongue and teeth.

It's been twenty-five years since snow machines hit the country. Common sense says that all game populations have to be declining. Still, the best guess by both biologists and Eskimos is that wolves in the northwest arctic are actually increasing along with the caribou herd; you can find wolf trails and kill remains a few miles from most villages. The blue-white ocean of land seems vast enough, for now, to bear the pressure.

It's an April morning, and Clarence is in his yard, packing his sled. He just got back from a long run through the Selawik valley, and already the village is too crowded for him.

"Where to, Clarence?"

"Noatak way. Douglas Creek, Maybe Nigu." The Nigu valley is 200 miles from here, part of an old sled dog route to Anaktuvuk Pass and the North Slope. Clarence is one of a few who still remembers the way.

"Going alone?" I ask, knowing the answer.

"Those Anaktuvuk guys say there's anymuch wolf there now."

An hour later he's off, heading north into deep cold, throttle wide open. From my classroom window, I have a fleeting vision of Clarence and a pack of wolves running together. I silently wish him good luck, then offer the wolves the same.

I had never known the country to be so barren as it was in those months. This mountainous wilderness was hardpacked with snow and downy with many flakes of frost. Not a living thing we found that we could kill for food.

The dried fish and berries were rationed among us, and we had one meal a day. Soon we were given as little as a couple handfuls of berries. I could see that everyone was losing weight. The clothes we wore hung loose on our bodies. Still we traveled north, not knowing that we might come back down this trail.

—from "Lights of the Caribou,"
in Lela Kiana Oman's *Eskimo Legends*

A Place Beyond

︿︿︿︿︿︿︿︿︿

T he Brooks Range, an old Eskimo man once told me, sings whatever you wish to hear. A lonely man might hear voices; a lost man, the sound of motors. I sat alone on a pinnacle overlooking the blue-white expanse of the upper Noatak valley, wondering what it was that I heard. It might have been wind on distant peaks except for an undertone—a soft, rhythmic thud that seemed to rise from everywhere. As the late winter sun warmed my face I scanned the sky, the mountains, and the tundra below, searching for the source. Only gradually did I realize that what filled my ears was the hiss of my own blood and the beating of my heart.

Across the valley, north to east, the surreal crags and spires of the Schwatkas loomed, and far to the south the Bairds rode the horizon like distant sails. Of the dozens of peaks before me, only a handful bore recorded names. Home, the village of Ambler, lay sixty miles to the southwest, walled off by a maze of limestone ridges and canyons that would double the traveling distance. There might be a trapper camped on the Nigu River, fifty miles to the north, but no marked trails led there, or to Ambler, or to anywhere else. I was alone.

I'd traveled this far by snowmobile with Clarence Wood. He'd packed his sled the day before, headed for Anaktuvuk Pass, and I'd decided to camp in the upper Noatak a few days and explore some of the smaller drainages leading toward the Kobuk divide, places seldom visited even by the Nunamiut wolf hunters—barren, dead-end valleys with ancient names: Natmaktugiaq, Kavachuraq, Tunukuchiaq.

"Pretty rough country," Clarence had said, and shrugged.

By the time I returned to my canvas tent, nestled in a clump of scrub willow, the valley had sunk into shadow and the temperature was falling fast. Although March in the arctic is a time of bright days and growing warmth, frost now clung to my eyelashes; pinprick tingles warned me the tip of my nose was freezing, as it always does near thirty below. I stoked the stove, and in minutes I was stripped down to long johns, steaming dry as supper cooked. Outside my island of warmth, creek ice groaned and cracked in the deepening cold, and the aurora flickered across the sky as if fanned by a great wind.

The Brooks Range. The words conjure up visions—jagged mountains and icewater rivers, grizzlies and caribou, fearsome cold, stunning beauty and vastness. Few places are broad enough to bear the weight of our dreams; the Brooks is one of them. Stretching across the state of Alaska, it remains one of the last great chunks of wild country anywhere—a mountain system over seven hundred miles long and up to a hundred wide, all above the arctic circle. Superimposed on a map of the Lower 48, the Brooks Range would stretch from Manhattan to the Mississippi.

Considered by many geologists to be the northernmost expression of the Rocky Mountains, the Brooks is divided into nine major and dozens of minor subranges, all linked by a common geological past. Roughly 160 million years ago, a slab of oceanic bedrock crushed into the north coast of Alaska, forcing the land upward. Twisted, tilted strata throughout the range bear witness to the unspeakable pressures of birth; ridges a mile high were once the floor of an ancient sea.

For all its vastness, the Brooks remains almost untouched by man. Native villages dot the southern flank of the range, and a few more sit on the oil-rich coastal plain known as the North Slope. But the tiny settlements within the Brooks Range proper are so scattered that they seem lost, adrift on a rolling ocean of land.

I awoke with a start. It was before dawn, and something was outside the tent. Burrowed in my sleeping bag, I lay tense as frost feathers melted on my face. There—the creak and rustle of footpads on snow. A wolverine? A grizzly just out of the den? I could hear my sled tarp rustling as whatever it was rummaged ten feet away. I wriggled into the cold and groped for my rifle. Lifting the tent flap, I met a pair of yellow eyes.

The red fox was less startled than I. He bounded off a few yards, then sat with head tilted, tail curled over his toes. We eyed each other, and then he rose, yawned, and resumed his patrol of my camp. As I warmed up and ate breakfast, the big male sniffed around. When I poked my head through the tent flap to watch, he regarded me with baffled interest. Finally he edged over to my snowmobile and nosed the ski. Then he lifted a leg and gave his reply.

Man has left two notable marks (some would say scars) on this country: the Trans-Alaska Pipeline and its haul road bisect the central Brooks, and, far to the west, the newly opened Red Dog mine, the second largest lead and zinc deposit in the world, is joined by road to a barge port on the arctic coast. Still, there is no forged link to the outside other than the pipeline road, two lanes of gravel completed more than twenty years ago.

That so much land remains so wild is scarcely an accident. Some ten thousand mining claims and known mineral deposits are scattered through the mountains, and easements exist for the railroads and highways of the future. But almost the entire Brooks Range, 35.2 million acres in all, has been preserved in an interconnected system of national monuments, parks, preserves, and wildlife refuges (including the Arctic National Wildlife Refuge) running from the Canadian border west to the Chukchi Sea. These protected lands are the fruits of an ongoing, sometimes bitter struggle.

Under the terms of the Alaska Native Claims Settlement Act of 1971, the federal government, the state, and Native groups sat down to divide the vast pie that was Alaska. The Brooks Range, country too remote and rugged to be of primary interest to the state or to most Native corporations, ended up on the federal side of the table.

But another ten years of legal wrangling passed before officials completed the transfer to the national park system. Powerful prodevelopment lobbies (led by oil and mineral interests and supported by many Alaskans) fought back every step of the way, forcing Interior Secretary Cecil Andrus and President Carter to rely on stopgap measures and legal loopholes to keep alive the vision of a protected Brooks Range. Finally, late in 1980 Carter signed into law the Alaska National Interest Lands Conservation Act. By that stroke of ink the National Park Service gained a hunk of Alaska the size of fifteen Yellowstones.

After surveying its new domain, the park service decided to do something unique with the Brooks Range: nothing. There would be no access roads, marked trails, campgrounds, gates, or signs. Native hunters and wolves would continue to roam over the landscape in search of caribou, free of scenic overlooks and rest areas. If outsiders chose to pass through, it would be on the land's terms. Except for several tiny ranger stations, the country would remain itself, a place beyond wilderness, a place to remember what had always been.

Dozens of narrow side valleys cut into the upper Noatak. From the main river many look the same, but each unfolds into a world of its own. Natmaktugiaq, with its rolling tundra and spectacular peaks, is a corridor for men and animals moving between the Noatak and the Ambler; the name, in fact, means "place to carry over." Its neighbor Tunukuchiaq runs into a canyon full of thin ice and boulders. I was headed up Kavachuraq, a valley, Clarence told me, where no one goes.

The day was calm, the glare of sun against the snow almost blinding. I rode slowly across a flat, scanning for movement. Ptarmigan chuckled in the willows, then erupted in a cloud as a gyrfalcon swooped over. Near a stretch of blue overflow there were fresh caribou tracks; two running wolf trails met them, and blood flecks led over the ridge. The valley narrowed and I entered a canyon, snaked along for several miles, then climbed out through a gully. Now the mountains seemed to hang overhead, and a shadowed chill hung in the air. Before me lay a snowfield, where the mountain walls had caught a winter's worth of snow and piled it ten feet deep. As I rode uphill in the half light, powder spraying about me, with no rock or twig to lend perspective, I was overwhelmed by the sensation of flight. I could see a dim edge ahead where the sky seemed to end.

Fifty yards from the cliff I cut my engine. Behind me the Kavachuraq wound northward; except for the thin curve of my trail, there was no sign that any living thing had ever been here. I stepped off my machine into a world without sound, without motion, where the only possible color was white.

Months later, sitting in my cabin, surrounded by familiar things, I listen to the hiss and crackle of the woodstove and find that my memories somehow have blurred. I remember crawling to the lip of a cornice and staring down a canyon wall that seemed to drop forever; I remember how the mountains rose above me in the twilight like great cold hands; I remember, too, that the snowfield felt like a dead place, and that wonder turned to discomfort, then suddenly gave way to fear; that I floundered back to my machine and roared down the valley, never looking back.

I recall these things, but they seem vague, rounded at the edges like dreams. I had seen places like Kavachuraq before, and had traveled hundreds, thousands of miles alone. I thought I knew this country, and perhaps I did; but I still don't understand that moment of panic, any more than I understand what I was running from—whether it was from the mountains themselves, or just from that place, or from the sound of my own heart beating in a silence that was too far and deep.

In September we went up to Kuugruaq or
Nimiuktuk. We pulled the skin boats upriver—
never used sails—used two or three dogs to
pull boat. Men pulled the boat while women
poled. . . . When we went home from hunting we
would get the boat and go back downriver.
If we didn't see any caribou we went as far as
the ocean (we could see the ocean when we climbed
the mountain—it looked like smoke). This trip
took a long time, maybe a month.

 We dried up the meat, fat and all, over a fire
and tried to carry it all back with us. The hunters
were using rifles and hunted like people do now.
If my father was lucky he might get four or five
caribou . . . but we usually didn't get lots and
sometimes didn't get any.

 . . . After we got to Naupaktusugruk the
Noatagmiut [lower Noatak people] came, traveling
the same way. . . . On the way some people always
throw those who starve or who are too weak
to go farther. They leave them on the trail.

—from the autobiography of
Edna Hunnicutt, *The Eskimo Storyteller*,
by Edwin S. Hall, Jr.

What They Leave Behind

▲▲▲▲▲▲▲▲▲

Around the middle of May, the sun has eaten most of the snow around Noatak village. It's a quiet time of year—endless days of dazzling light and growing warmth, the sky dotted with returning ducks and geese, a dreamlike blue cast to the mountains. The white land sags inward, and whatever lay hidden for months reappears. Anything dark is a heat sink, and circles of thawing spread outward from lost gloves, torn snow machine belts, trash bags. All around the village, the winter's flotsam and jetsam washes up on the shores of spring. It's not the prettiest time of year if you look down too much.

Away from town—out goose hunting, say—is another story. There, the dark things that eat snow are rocks, twigs, spruce needles. But in town, it's trash. You get to see and smell exactly how much of a mess 350 people can make over a winter. For eight months, everyone has taken nature's icebox and the camouflage of snow for granted, and every year the thaw is so sudden that everyone seems caught by surprise. It's time to clean out the cache—fast—and spruce up the dooryard, haul things to the dump with the snow machine before the snow is gone, and before certain things get too soft to handle. Although just about everyone makes regular dump runs all winter long, most households have a pretty good pile—a few sledloads, anyway—to haul now, in the last week before breakup.

The dump is about a mile south of town, out past the airstrip and the sewage lagoon. All it is, really, is a clearing about a quarter mile long and a few hundred yards wide. It's surrounded by a stand of stunted white spruce. On one side is the riverbank, a stone's throw away, and on the other is a stretch of tundra and lakes rising into the Mulgrave Hills. The nearest highway, the pipeline haul road, is 300 miles east. The trail runs lengthwise between the river and the dump. There are no fences, no signs, no posted rules. Just pull up and throw your stuff by the roadside. Every few months, the town bulldozer, or Cat, pushes everything back into piles, and sometimes the piles are burned.

It's hard to tell just where the dump ends and the country begins. Trash bags break open on the way or fall from sleds, or someone in a hurry dumps their load halfway there. The wind scatters paper; loose dogs from the village, foxes, and the odd bear rummage around; the ravens, always watching and waiting, do their part. There's not so much of a Noatak dump as a general dumping zone, rubble radiating outward from ground zero as if a huge trash bomb had fallen from the sky.

The village of Noatak has only existed for eighty years or so as a permanent settlement, and the current dump is less than half that old. Thirty years ago, there was far less stuff to throw away (even with almost the same population), and another thirty years before that, less again. A dump is a pretty reliable gauge of the standard of living; you can tell a lot about a people by what they can afford to throw away.

For at least 2,000 years, the Inupiat managed to survive with a technology based on subsistence. The land provided virtually all of their needs: skins for clothing, footwear, tents, containers, and boat coverings; wood, bone, stone, and ivory for tools and weapons; birds, mammals, fish, and plants for food. They built *ebruliks* (houses) of sod and spruce poles, and warmed them with seal oil lamps or wood. The Inupiat did trade to supplement what they had—with Siberian Eskimos, Koyukuk River Indians, and later, with explorers, miners, and whalers—but they could usually do without.

By necessity, they were a frugal people; amassing a pile of nonconsumables was pointless. With the land providing nearly everything, wealth was not a relevant concept, and the Inupiat focused on the practical. They had to travel quickly and lightly, long distances over rough terrain, often racing the weather, walking, paddling, and using dogs to pull boats and sleds. They hunted and gathered as they went, true opportunists. If they came across a needed resource—

berries, ptarmigan, a useful chunk of spruce—they utilized it and moved on.

Not surprisingly, the early Inupiat left little behind to mark their passing. They didn't even bury their dead, but left them on the tundra, covered with caribou skins, or inside a teepee of spruce poles. Everything they had, except for some ivory, stone, and the odd piece of bone, returned to the land within a few years: wood and hide rotted, and empty sod houses, unmaintained, soon wore away in the wind and rain, leaving only rounded depressions.

Nobody made any serious attempt to unearth the Inupiat past until a young archeologist named Louis Giddings came to the northwest arctic in the 1940s. He covered vast areas of the Kobuk and Noatak valleys on foot, traveling light and moving along waterways, like the people whose leavings he sought. He traveled alone, carried no gun and little food; when he wanted to cross a river, he swam or built a raft. Giddings found winter house pits at caribou crossings and at tributary confluences, marked them, and walked on. In excavations during the 1950s and '60s at sites like Onion Portage on the upper Kobuk River and Cape Krusenstern on the coast northwest of Noatak, Giddings and his assistants found tiny scraps of arctic civilization going back 10,000 years. There was never much to go on: small bone fragments around excavated hearths, surprisingly small and delicate stone fragments from weapons and tools.

These long-gone peoples were labeled in the only logical manner, after what was found and where: the Denbigh Flint complex, the Arctic Small Tools tradition, and so on. But they were not Eskimos in their toolmaking technology. In strata dating around 1800 B.C., at Cape Krusenstern, Giddings found the first signs of Eskimo-like peoples, which, from their tools and bone fragments of prey, he labeled the Old Whaling culture. These people left more and larger signs of their passing: bigger house pits, bigger tool fragments, more bones of larger mammals (including whales and walrus), shards of pottery and slate. Unlike the earlier peoples, these whalers left signs of having work dogs—harness pieces, sled fragments, and bones. In other digs, there was evidence of other Eskimo subtraditions. What seemed to connect all of them was a trend toward similar, bigger tools.

But now it's late May, a warm, sunny afternoon at the Noatak dump, and the snow is going fast. The refuse of an entire winter—eight months' worth—is resurfacing, and there is the pile of last-minute trash besides. As I pull up on my snow machine, the ravens, twenty or so, rise reluctantly, flap to nearby treetops and wait, squawking hoarsely. What I'm about to do isn't much different from what archeologists do: go through peoples' old trash to see what they've been up to. Of course, it's a little different from archeology here—this is more immediate, as a glance and a sniff will tell you. And my methods are less refined. I'm more like a paparazzo rummaging through a movie star's garbage than a scientist systematically probing downward, carefully sifting through the remains of a vanished civilization. Unlike an archeologist, I need rubber boots and a reasonably steady stomach.

At first glance, it's like a dump anywhere—dark plastic trash bags, cardboard boxes, a few broken appliances, a rusted truck frame, and endless mounds of cans, bottles, and paper. But here's a rib cage with shards of greenish flesh clinging to it, and there's an antlered skull. There's a pile of small, skinned-out carcasses in a cardboard box. Hooves. Antlers. Unidentifiable haunches. Crushed heads. Hides slimy on the undersides, maggot-ridden. All are tattered and marked with the peck marks and droppings of the ravens. There must be hundreds of dead animals here, maybe a thousand if you dug under the piles of more ordinary trash—the cola cans, diapers, pickle jars, and so on. Someone who knows animals could give names to most of the fragments: caribou, wolf, fox, Dall sheep, moose, lynx, wolverine, snowshoe hare, ptarmigan, otter, dog, trout, salmon, grizzly bear. Death is everywhere. This isn't a dump. It's an animal Buchenwald. Animal rights advocates would be sick to their stomachs. There's more than just bones here; there are entire caribou haunches and unskinned foxes rotting and bloating with fly larvae in the May sun, wasted.

This dump isn't anything special. If you visited any of the ten village dumps in the region, you'd see more or less the same things. Maybe there would be more seal parts in the Kivalina and Deering dumps, and more wolf carcasses in Noatak than in Noorvik. But there would be the remains of thousands of animals. If you traveled across the length and breadth of Alaska, you'd see as many variations on the basic theme as there are villages. There are more than a hundred villages. Bush Alaska is a land of carnivores and predators, and unlike those in the Lower 48, the people, Native or white, don't buy most of their meat in supermarkets. Here you handle your own slaughterhouse offal, and it's disposed of closer to home.

Alongside the animal parts lie the skeletal snow machine bodies and the dead outboard motor fragments. There is a direct relationship between the machine and the animal carcasses: the machines give the mobility needed to procure the animals, with an ease and in a quantity the old *Napaaqtugmiut* could not have dreamed of.

There's more evidence of the new ways: a .30-06 Remington ammunition box here, a battered rifle scope there; lots of empty oil drums and rusted five-gallon gas cans; a broken basket sled made of hardwood grown thousands of miles to the south; an Eddie Bauer down jacket missing only a zipper, better than the one I'm wearing. There are torn hip waders, broken fishing reels, shotgun shell husks, ripped gillnets and seines, felt-lined boots; a stripped down Homelite chain saw. It's all mixed in with the animals, the disposable diapers, the many, many liquor bottles and candy wrappers, the bed frames, the empty containers and cans—Lysol, Hormel chili, Cheerios, Wesson Oil, eggs, Oreos, Seven-Up.

Watch where you step: those hundreds of formless, plastic trash sacks are thawing, and they contain abundant evidence that the village sewer system froze solid (as usual) sometime this winter, necessitating a return to honey buckets. All the scraps of high-tech insulated Arctic Pipe show that water and sewer exists, but at great cost and at the whim of nature.

What we have at the Noatak dump is perhaps unique in world history: evidence of a high-tech hunter-gatherer society. This is more than Amazonian Indians with transistor radios and Michael Jackson T-shirts. That sort of overlapping is almost universal in the Third World, and passé to cultural anthropologists. The Mindi of New Guinea and the Masai of east Africa may have a few trappings of modern technology—wrist watches or jogging shoes—but nothing like the wealth and variety represented by the contents of the Noatak dump. These Eskimos have their feet solidly planted in two worlds. On second thought, maybe it's more like one foot is on a dock, the other on a departing boat. They use Ziploc bags to store beluga whale *muktuq*. They play Nintendo, then get up to go wolf hunting, ride $5,000 iron dogs through mountain passes their ancestors traversed with sleds.

Aarigaa, pretty soon fresh caribou soup. I sure miss that kind. When it's fall time, caribous start crossing and we always get lots.

It's tempting to simplify things, to say that these people are obviously part of the cash economy, and affluent enough that they don't need the land any longer. Let them buy pork chops and Banquet chicken dinners like civilized folks instead of slaughtering caribou and seals, despoiling the last wilderness in North America. But the *Napaaqtugmiut* are not playing at subsistence, going through the motions out of habit or mere preference. All households do have some sort of cash income, be it from commerical fishing, union construction work, a job at the local school, or welfare. Some families make $30,000 or $40,000 a year. They also get yearly dividends from NANA, the local Native corporation, plus free medical care from the Public Health Service, and heavily subsidized housing. They get unemployment checks, Alaska Permanent Fund checks, and food stamps, too.

Without the land's gifts, though, it's not enough—in any sense. If you walk into any home around mealtime, you'll see canned peas, Sailor Boy pilot bread (unleavened, large round crackers—a staple), coffee, maybe Campbell's soup, and other "store food," as they call it. You'll also see a caribou haunch, or a frozen raw trout with bowls of seal oil (*usruq,* the universal condiment), dried salmon, beluga *muktuq,* duck soup, or moose nose. There will be berries for dessert, or maybe *akutuq,* Eskimo ice cream: whipped fat blended with berries, sugar, and boiled fish. What's on the table depends on what season it is, and on the luck of the hunters. But the main course, as well as some of the side dishes, will be food from the land.

> When I was working in Fairbanks I sure miss Eskimo food. If you eat store food only, you can't get full.
>
> ———
>
> That one time schooling in Oklahoma, I turned kind of white or pale from weak food. Just like you! When I got back, my grandma let me eat good Eskimo food, and pretty soon I get brown and healthy again.
>
> ———
>
> If I don't go hunt, pretty soon I can't do nothing. Get lazy, start drinking. When I hunt, I'm a real Eskimo.

Subsistence is more than a matter of dietary preference or spiritual well-being. With gas near $3.00 a gallon, a winter week's worth of fuel oil $50.00, a pound of hamburger $4.89 (when they can get it), money doesn't go very far. Some of the families could probably survive physically on store food. Some would just about starve, food stamps or no.

It's true that there are televisions, cola cans, and other nonessentials at the dump, but how can we begrudge the Inupiat the same excesses and comforts we enjoy? Life is bleak enough in the arctic winters as it is; the suicide rate in the Alaskan bush is the highest in the nation. But ask one of the elders if the old ways were better, or if they were enough.

> Back then, too hard. Always working. People always dying. Too much funeral. Now I have sixteen grandchildren, and all living. *Aarigaa*— that's good.

The Inupiat have always lived in the present, in a way many whites find inexplicable. You have to think what an archeologist a thousand years from now would make of what this latest version of arctic man has left behind. The Denbigh Flint people, the Old Whaling tradition, and the others took what they needed from the land, and most of it returned in due time, without a trace. There was no such thing as littering. Space age plastics and aluminum are another story. They don't go away.

This fact is slowly sinking in with the *Napaaqtugmiut.* Out on the river, many heave their empty pop cans overboard casually, or even with unmistakable gusto, as if the act of littering affirms their dominance over the land or signifies a ritual marking of territory. Some hunters leave trash out in the middle of nowhere, where it flutters in the wind year after year. They leave empty gas cans, laugh and call them "trail markers" if you ask why. I've often found myself sneaking along behind companions, surreptitiously picking up their cans and plastic, embarrassed when I'm discovered. I can never bring myself to ask them not to drop their trash by the trail, as they always have. Who am I to impose my own standards?

Other Eskimos, though, pick up candy wrappers and keep their fish camps clean. Most litter is swept seaward by high water, or lost in the vast ocean of land.

What we call trash is a matter of opinion. I was walking in the hills with an older Noatak man, far up a small, nameless valley. The mountains loomed over us on both sides, looking as they must have a thousand years ago. Following the creek bed, we came on a few rusted cans marking an old camp. Someone had stopped here, maybe twenty years before.

"Aarigaa," said my friend. "Now it doesn't seem so lonely."

It is said that when [Tikigilaq] decided that he wanted to go up the Kobuk River while he was still down there on the coast, he swam up with the sheefish. He [his spirit] went inside the body of a sheefish. As the sheefish journeyed up the river, they often got caught in seining nets. As it was, the two sheefish who were his tukkuq *(meaning host of a visitor or the one that a visitor or traveller stays with) lifted the net aside each time they were caught so that Tikigilaq would not get caught. They did this every time there was a seining net blocking the way. Each time they did this, Tikigilaq swam below the net and escaped. That was how he had the sheefish help him journey up the river.*

It is said that he carefully observed the people seining each time in hopes of finding a woman to be born from. Each time he didn't find anyone to stay in, he escaped. This happened until they reached people seining way up along the Upper Kobuk. There he saw a tiny woman whose interior was very becoming. It was bright inside her. Because he liked what he saw, he decided to stop there. He allowed himself to be caught in the seining net and as they were about to work on the sheefish, he moved from the sheefish and into the woman. Thus, he had found a mother.

—Robert Nasruk Cleveland and Donald Foote,
Stories of the Black River People

Sheefish Time

▲▲▲▲▲▲▲▲▲

After a hundred casts, I'd stopped thinking; I drifted off into the rhythm of cast and retrieve as the Kobuk River flowed by in the bright arctic midnight. The water was low and clear, dimpled by rising grayling. I was after something bigger—sheefish, a race of giant whitefish that inhabits only a few dozen river systems in northern Alaska, Canada, and Siberia. Here in the remote Kobuk and neighboring Selawik drainages, the fish are arguably the largest anywhere. Twenty to thirty pounders are common, and the world all-tackle record of fifty-three pounds, caught in 1986, came from the upper Kobuk.

I was anchored at the edge of an eddy, where the current spilled off a bar and pooled green. I'd caught fish here several times over the years, and I'd already seen a couple rolling on the surface tonight. But sheefish are moody; they might refuse to strike for hours, even days. Then again, they might suddenly erupt into a frenzy—especially late on a clear July night. And so I cast again and again, waiting. I could feel the *tap-tap-tap* of my heavy spoon brushing the sandy bottom, and its flutter as I jigged it upward. If a strike came, it would be on the settle. If not, I'd cast again.

Here, at the edge of the western Brooks Range, time isn't measured in hours and minutes; there are other rhythms, larger and less definite. Part of being here is learning to empty yourself of clocks, to see time as it's measured by the land—an endless pattern of cycles and momentary abundances. There's a time when blueberries ripen, another for caribou to migrate. This was the time when sheefish run upriver. They were here, and so was I. That was all I needed to know.

I was paying attention to something else—the Jade Mountains

reflecting the evening sun, or a widgeon paddling by—when it came. There was the thrum of my lure working as it swung in the current, the occasional tap of the bottom, then an electric *tugtugtug WHAM,* and my line and heart were singing with the rod's bow. Ten yards out, there was the bright bulge of a fish coming up, and a boil the size of a washtub—a big female, broad and heavy with eggs. Her tail and backfin thrashed against the sharp weight in her mouth, and she exploded downstream, hissing my line away, fifteen-pound test barely enough to take the pressure. Twenty yards. Thirty. Finally I brought her back, pumping and reeling, giving line when she ran, until I had her under the boat. As I reached for the gaff, she made a last surge for the bottom, nearly taking my rod. At last I got the lower jaw and hoisted her aboard—a bright, bucket-mouthed fish of twenty pounds.

I looked up to the mountains, out over the tundra, and downriver, where clouds were turning the color of blood. The willows caught the wind, bowed and flashed silver, and a flight of mergansers whistled overhead without swerving.

Sheefish have always been creatures of mystery; early French-Canadian explorers called them *poissons inconnus,* unknown fish. Only in the past twenty years have biologists, notably Ken Alt of the Alaska Department of Fish and Game, filled most of the gaps in our knowledge. Still, sheefish refuse man's attempts to breed them successfully in hatcheries.

In both appearance and habit, sheefish seem to be a mongrel blend of species. They've been called "tarpon of the north" often enough that the comparison has become stale; true, they're big, square-jawed and silvery, and leap when hooked. But sheefish also run up rivers to spawn, as salmon do. Their voracious, predatory instincts seem to be borrowed from pike or bass. On the table, the rich, delicate, pinkish-white flesh tastes like a cross between halibut, trout, and crab. Only the fins are all whitefish.

Because sheefish are constantly on the move, finding them is most of the battle. Most sheefish migrate each spring from their winter homes in brackish estuaries to spawn in clear, swift river currents far upstream. Kobuk River sheefish, for example, swim as much as three hundred miles to their spawning beds near the Pah River. The run starts after the ice breaks up in late May or early June, and fish gradually work their way upstream until they reach the spawning grounds by late August. They don't dig redds (spawning beds) as salmon do, but broadcast their eggs over clean gravel as the males add milt. A thirty-pound female (the males are half as large) may drop 350,000 eggs. After spawning, the fish run downstream with the first ice floes to winter in Hotham Inlet, an arm of the Chukchi Sea. There they gorge on ciscos and smelt, fattening up for next year's run. Along with king salmon, they are among the largest and longest lived anadromous species; they may swim for twenty years.

Traditionally, the Inupiat seined for sheefish in the summer as the fish made their way upriver, and dangled hooks made of bear teeth and ivory through holes in the ice in winter. The rich, oily flesh and eggs of spawning females were especially prized as food for both people and dog teams. In early fall, whole fresh fish were buried ungutted in a leaf-lined pit to age several weeks. This "stink fish," eaten raw, had a cheeselike texture and a certain aroma that made it a special delicacy. In the past twenty years, rod and reel fishing has become the favored method for harvesting sheefish, especially among the upper Kobuk Eskimos.

Although sheefish as a rule don't feed in fresh water, they'll hit a well-presented lure at any time of year—if the water's clear enough, and if they're in the mood. Most fish lie deep through the day, moving little and refusing all offerings. In the late evening they begin to stir. Some continue their journey upstream, while others cruise along dropoffs or gravelly runs, rolling on the surface now and then. Eskimo anglers on the Kobuk usually start fishing around midnight, warming up with a fire and coffee when the action slows.

On a good night, you don't need a fire to keep warm. I recall a July evening twelve years ago, fishing a deep pool downstream from Ambler. I rode the thirty miles with two Eskimo friends in their plywood skiff. Low clouds scudded overhead, spattering rain. When we reached the spot, two other boats from the village were already pulled against the steep gravel beach. We waved—everybody knows everybody here—and rigged our rods. A hundred yards upstream, one man was leaning back, his rod bent double. Half-watching as I tied on, I saw him beach what looked like a silver log. I tossed my two-ounce Krocodile fifty yards into the current, counted as it sank, and began a slow jerk and flutter retrieve. *Whunk.* Something slammed in, tore off downstream, and snapped my line in one rush. Hands shaking, I reeled in what was left, tied on a new lure, and remembered to set my drag this time. Two casts later, I landed a fifteen pounder, and nailed its twin on the next try. Up and down the beach, everyone was catching fish. I cast again, felt a tap, and set the hook. The next thing I knew I was running down the beach, reel screeching, trying to save line.

Three hours later, the action ended as if someone had thrown a switch. Had the fish moved off or just stopped striking? The river flowed past, smooth and gray in the mist. My arms were wooden, my back drenched in sweat as I collected my fish and carried them two at a time to the boat. I'd kept six and released over a dozen, the smallest ten pounds, the largest somewhere between thirty-five and forty.

As we skimmed upstream toward home, the sun filtered through the fog, casting the world in silver light. "What time is it?" one of my friends asked. I looked down at the boat bottom, bright with fish. The light, diffused and timeless, seemed to flow from them. Sheefish time, I whispered to myself.

The anjatkut *stood her soul on his drum and it kept falling. The soul was a small thing, something like a crust of bread and kind of darkish in color, maybe shaped like a little doll. He started using a drum, and after he played it the cover would always come off. He put it back on and played it again. He kept playing it and when the cover didn't come off anymore he tried to inhale something. He had it in his mouth for awhile, and then he took it out and set it on the drum. It was* inuksuk, *her soul. A lot of people were around watching. It fell and he put it back up. It was falling because the woman was dying. Finally the soul stood up by itself. It started going around, jumping by itself, all over the drum. The* anjatkut *got ahold of it and put it on the dying woman's head. Then it went into her and they didn't see it anymore. The woman became alive.*

. . . Carl Luther's uncle had an anjatkut *[meaning in this context, a familiar relationship] with dogs and with the devil himself. When she got well he used the woman.*

—from the autobiography of
    Edna Hunnicutt, *The Eskimo Storyteller,*
    by Edwin S. Hall, Jr.

The Old Man's Winter

▲▲▲▲▲▲▲▲▲

Mark Cleveland sits on his porch steps in Ambler, remembering the first airplane he ever saw. "Up at Kobuk, around 1930s. It was springtime, maybe April. We hear it from long ways off, some kind of motor all right, but we don't know what it is. Then we see it, coming in low. Two wings, like this—" his hands become a biplane. "It landed on the ice in front of town. First time we see that kind. We sure look!" Mark laughs, his white hair haloed in the sun.

He stares off across the river. "Maniilaq knew it would happen like that," he nods, and looks straight into my eyes, as if challenging me to disbelieve. "White men coming from the east, riding up in the sky. That old man always knew everything."

That old man. People often refer to him without using his name, Maniilaq, which, roughly translated, means "rocky cliffs." There is a mountain called that above Kobuk village, not far from the place where he was born. That dark, ragged heap of basalt rises over dozens of lesser peaks, looking as though it fell from the moon. I'm not sure whether the mountain lent its name to the man or vice versa, but either way it's a fitting monument to a figure who loomed over the human landscape of his time. Maniilaq—a wandering holy man who saw The People's future and led them toward it, risking death and ignoring ridicule. Some say he was the voice of God.

After years of hearing snatches of tales, unsure what to believe myself, I set out in search of Maniilaq and his real story. But the further I dug, the more I found myself caught up in a world beyond facts.

This much is certain: Maniilaq was once flesh and blood. Perhaps a third of the upper Kobuk people can trace their family trees back to him; elders like Clara Lee can recite dozens of names, starting with Maniilaq's mother and working forward to the present through a maze of uncles, cousins, and siblings:

> [Maniilaq's] mother was Qupilguuraq. [Maniilaq] was the eldest. His younger sisters were Imgusriq, Qapuluk and Sinaana. As far as I know, Itluun was the name of his son. He also had a daughter. . . . As for Imgusriq, her children were Qapqauraq, Qaksri and Paniyaq. . . .

A surprising amount is known of Maniilaq's life, thanks to an oral tradition that, for centuries, took the place of a written language. Now television, radio, and books are the storytellers, and most of those who remember the old ways are gone. But some of their heritage was rescued over the last four decades, partly by the 1978 NANA Region Elders Conference dedicated to Maniilaq. The accounts recorded there form a remarkable document—a web of memories stretched across time, bearing witness to a man whose vision of the future continues to unfold as he predicted.

Charlie Aqpaliq Sheldon admonishes, "We are attempting to speak about something of importance, something that our descendants will experience. Although what we say today will seem new to us, it will become as a legend in the future. . . . Whatever we experienced yesterday has become history. . . . Our meeting now will be history tomorrow."

Susie Anigniq Stocking, frail and ancient, struggling to remember, apologizes to everyone: "You see, I do not know everything. It seems that I am merely an ordinary person."

The elegance and restraint of these voices reverberate, their poignancy magnified by the fact that most of those who spoke at the conference are now dead. It doesn't matter what you believe; these accounts, transcribed word for word in the elevated style of formal Inupiaq, come from the heart of The People. Maniilaq's story is their own, one that reminds them of who they are.

Maniilaq was born in the early 1800s near a place called Qala, not far from the present village of Kobuk. He and three younger sisters were raised by their mother, Qupilguuraq. As the eldest child in a fatherless household, responsibility came early to Maniilaq. He helped to build their winter sod house and became adept at snaring rabbits and ptarmigan, often going out alone. As he rested in the woods one day, a small bird spoke to him. *"Taatagiik, taatagiik,"* it called—"Father and son, father and son." Mesmerized, the young Maniilaq returned to the place many times, and sometimes sat all day, listening, filled with a strange, radiant calm. Soon the message became *"Taatagiik, taatagiik. Isrummiqsuqti, isrummiqsuqti"*—"Father and son, father and son, the source of intelligence, the source of thought." When he finally told his mother about the bird, she worried that he was becoming an *anjatkut,* a shaman, one who moved between the worlds of spirits and men. He reassured her, and went on listening.

As Maniilaq grew into a young man, his "source of intelligence" guided his thoughts. He found he could catch any animal he wished, and he obeyed when his inner voice chose a wife for him. For a time, he and his family lived peacefully. But, although he kept to himself, others began to notice what Beatrice Mouse calls "the brilliant light within him." Inevitably, the *anjatkut* sought him out, demanding he show them his powers.

The Inupiat of the northwest arctic had no true religion, no deities or rituals of worship. Yet they had a profound belief in the supernatural which verged on dread. The land swarmed with spirits *(tuungak)* and ghosts *(piinjilak),* all potentially hostile. Even normal actions, performed improperly, could bring illness or death to an entire camp. Any bad fortune—from poor hunting to difficulty bearing children—had its roots in *spiritus mundi.* To protect themselves, The People observed an elaborate system of taboos. An upper Kobuk man named Kahkik told anthropologist Louis Giddings, "Those people think if they cut a piece of caribou skin during fishing season and tan it, they will die. . . . When the moon gets dark those people, if they forget and leave food out in the cache, they have to throw it away."

In such a world, the *anjatkut* reigned supreme. Only they had the power to intercede with the spirits, warn of invisible dangers, and offer protection to ordinary people. With the help of *kila* (familiars) and the *tuungak* (spirits) themselves, *anjatkut* could travel by astral projection into the world beyond and set things right. The most powerful among them flew to the moon and waged fierce, sometimes fatal battles with other shamans. Some *anjatkut* were evil, and killed people; others were healers. The services of either were available for a price. Payment might be in furs, meat, the favors of a daughter, or obedience to a special taboo.

Disobeying or showing disrespect to an *anjatkut* was unthinkable; when a group of these men challenged Maniilaq, he should have been terrified. Beatrice Mouse, 87 years old herself in 1978, remembers what her mother told her as a child:

> The people of Qala and Suluppuaugaqtuuq gathered together at Paa. . . . [They] had heard, with apparent disbelief, about Maniilaq referring to his "source of intelligence." When they had gathered, Maniilaq appeared calm as he rested in a prone position and told the *anjatkut* to go ahead and summon their spirits. He did not become uncomfortable as the *anjatkut* chanted their incantations and performed their rituals. . . . They sang all night long, offering oil and food into a fire. . . . In the meantime, Maniilaq remained calm and undisturbed.
>
> When they were done, they turned to him and sarcastically asked him, "What is the matter? Are you too frightened to speak? Are you afraid now? Why don't you talk about the one you are always referring to as your source of intelligence?" There were many who taunted him and ridiculed him.
>
> Finally, he stood up and began to pace in a circle. *"Hi, hiii! Yaiy!"* he exclaimed, adding, "My dear source of intelligence, you have blessed me with another day. . . ." Mother was among those sitting on the floor who saw and heard him as he paced in a circle and spoke in front of the audience. Once again he exclaimed, *"Hi hii,* you all will come to know and understand my source of intelligence. However, it does not matter what I say now. You will not comprehend my meaning." That is what he said to them, adding, "When the necessities of life become easier to obtain and survival becomes easier, then you will understand. . . . Even the practice itself of being an *anjatkut* shall disappear."

Enraged at this impertinence, the *anjatkut* stalked off into the darkness. The watchers soon followed, certain that Maniilaq would be dead by morning. But he and his family went home to bed as if nothing had happened.

The elders tell how, later that night, the *anjatkut* returned, traveling in their astral forms, intent on "swallowing" Maniilaq's soul. They searched for it, but they found themselves blinded by an intense glow that surrounded his home. They groped about all night, murder in their hearts, searching for an opening to squeeze through. All the while, Maniilaq and his family slept peacefully behind their shield of light.

This was the first of dozens of attempts that the *anjatkut* made on Maniilaq's life. His lack of fear was insulting, his defiance unsettling. Singly and in groups they tried to "swallow" him, but the elders say that even the most powerful, Ayaunigruaq and Tuuyuq, could not penetrate his brilliant aura. In a celebrated confrontation near present-day Kotzebue, Maniilaq told these *anjatkut* he could "swallow" *them* if he wished, and still no harm came to him. As this news spread, people began to nod when Maniilaq's name was mentioned.

Now he traveled up and down the Kobuk like an Old Testament prophet, covering huge distances by foot, kayak, and dogsled, defying local shamans, making bold predictions. Often he'd pull into a camp, settle in, and deliberately break whatever deadly taboo presented itself—scraping animal hides during the summer, or mixing beluga *muqtuq* (blubber) with berries in the same meal. People watched incredulously and sometimes fled in panic, sure that he and his children, who often accompanied him, would be struck dead. When he'd appear again, the next day, healthy and unharmed, they feared him all the more. It was as if they'd seen someone fall from a great height and simply walk away.

The elders insist that Maniilaq was doing far more than quashing empty superstitions. Both Charlie Sheldon and Kahkik are careful to point out that people *did* die from taboo violations before Maniilaq interceded. Mark Cleveland makes the same point when I ask him if he thinks Maniilaq changed what happened or just what the people believed. "What happened," Mark says emphatically. "Before, someone would die. Maniilaq changed that. But even now, I never work with skins in summertime. Not many people here will. After fishing is done, it's okay again, we start sewing."

"But if Maniilaq made it all right, why follow a superstition?"

Mark pauses, then grins like an elf. "Just making sure."

Some of the harshest taboos were directed toward women, who were considered inferior from birth. When a girl reached puberty, she was forced to live alone for a year in a hut built by her parents. Forbidden to look upon men, she had to hide her face even from her mother. Beatrice Mouse remembers:

> When traveling up the river to a camp where a girl was in isolation, it was difficult to stay away, especially if she happened to be your best friend. On one such occasion, I brought some seal oil and berries to my friend, who was in isolation, and she burst into tears. What a pity it was when these girls were sometimes kept hungry.

Women were also shunned during their periods, and widows were declared carriers of contagion. The most stringent taboo of all, though, was directed at pregnant women. Even in the depths of winter, a woman in labor was expected to stagger into the woods and give birth alone; no one could help her without fear of contamination. Friends might build a fire for her and lay down a caribou hide, but that was all. After she'd had her child, she crawled to a snow shelter that had already been prepared, where she would stay for ten days, and then move to yet another hut before she could return home. If her infant was a girl, it might be cast out and left to die.

Maniilaq attacked these dictums hardest of all. He said that women were more precious than men and deserved tender care rather than cruelty, that such barbarism would be unthinkable in the future. And though these taboos outlasted Maniilaq by a generation, they slowly faded out.

Although Maniilaq's reputation was spreading, many people still ridiculed him. Others kept their distance, and with good reason: his actions as well as his words marked him as a madman. Not only did he bathe regularly and sleep on willow branches; everywhere he went he carried a long pole which he would raise when he made camp. At regular intervals (some claim every seventh day) he would tie something— elders disagree what it was—to his pole as a signal for people to gather. On these days he would refuse to travel or hunt; instead, he'd beat his skin drum, sing, and make his predictions to anyone who would listen.

The *iivaqsaat* (literally, those who travel around bends in waterways) were coming. These pale-skinned strangers, Maniilaq said, would ride out of the east, traveling in swift boats and fire-powered chairs in the sky. They'd bring many wonders to The People: thin birch bark on which to write, a way to contain fire inside houses, and the ability to speak across great distances. A large city would grow at the mouth of the Ambler River, where the *iivaqsaat* would seek something of great value in the earth. Mark Cleveland insists that one day the village will become a city stretching all the way to the Jade Mountains, eight miles away.

And, Maniilaq said, "Light will come in the form of the word"— one of many obvious references to Christianity, which arrived with Friends Church missionaries just before the turn of the century. He spoke, too, of a "grandfather" whose glorious power would soon be seen. Hearing of Maniilaq, the missionaries were quick to adopt him (posthumously, of course) as a prophet of God—a move that no doubt hastened their acceptance, even as it confirmed Maniilaq's stature.

As I read through the accounts of the dead, as I look into Mark Cleveland's earnest face, I want to share the belief that I find there. But I can't help insisting, deep down, on a logical explanation for Maniilaq and his visions. He certainly was a man of intelligence and courage, and I don't begrudge him a certain prescience—one born of rational thought. Defying the shamans and their taboos wasn't magic, I tell myself, just a triumph of common sense. It's likely he'd heard of white men and their God through travelers from the south. The Russians were trading on the Yukon River a century before Maniilaq was born, and Otto von Kotzebue, a Russian naval officer who explored the northwest arctic coast in 1816, saw iron knives among the Inupiat, showing that contact already existed with the outside world. Yet I can't explain how a nineteenth-century Eskimo envisioned outboard motors, aircraft, and telephones decades before their invention, or how he saw Ambler a century before its founding. When I offer elders my logical version, they only shake their heads. How can a *naluaqmiu* understand?

Not all of Maniilaq's predictions have come to pass. Elders speak of an equal number awaiting fulfillment, and many of these are tinged with darkness. There will be two consecutive winters, they say, when the snow will reach the treetops and a great famine will occur. A whale will surface on the upper Kobuk, and finally a day will come that appears to be split in half. When asked what lay beyond that day, Maniilaq is reported to have said, "All the people—I don't know what they are going to do, all the people."

While the old people offer little speculation on these last prophecies, they all agree with Susie Stocking:

> Now, we can see that Maniilaq's predictions have been fulfilled. We, ourselves, have lived through the changes and have seen his words come true . . . the rest will come. It will not fail to be fulfilled. The one who told about the future of the world has already predicted it.

Nothing, it seems, can surprise these people more than what they have already witnessed. "Just like the Bible," one tells me. "That old man can't miss."

Somewhere before the turn of the century, perhaps a decade before the missionaries, miners, and traders poured into the Kobuk valley, Maniilaq disappeared. He was last seen at the mouth of a slough called Tunnuuraq, where Ambler stands today. They say he headed north, an old man traveling alone through the mountains, across Anaktuvuk Pass to Barrow, then eastward toward Canada, dragging his pole and beating his drum for whoever would listen. Some say he died on the trail; Maniilaq claimed his body would not be found on earth, and that his pole would mark his place of departure. Neither a pole nor a body has ever been found; it's as if he rode his sled off the edge of the earth.

Maniilaq is gone, but his children remain. I teach them in school, trade jokes with them at the post office, and ride with them through the sky. I suppose I'm one of Maniilaq's children, too—one of the *iivaqsaat* who arrived one day, holding out the future. Now together we bear its weight. Somehow it's easiest for the elders, who watched it all happen. There is a serenity about them as they sit in church, nodding together. They lived hard, good lives, rooted in the traditions of Inupiaq; this strange new world bemuses them, but they're still sure of who they are.

But what about the young men who call city league basketball a career, or the dozens of young mothers living on welfare? In a very real sense, the struggle between Maniilaq and the shamans hasn't stopped. Now the new *anjatkut* of alcohol, television, and consumer goods exact their price of obedience. Doing figurative battle against them is the Maniilaq Association, a branch of NANA usually known simply as Maniilaq: a bureaucracy offering free health care, food stamps, counseling programs, and myriad other services—infant nutrition, cultural awareness, summer jobs, housing, even help with vegetable gardens. Beneath layers of irony lies a question: are these *naluaqmiut*-sponsored services the embodiment of the "easy" future the original Maniilaq predicted or the source of his despair?

Fourteen years ago, on that first canoe trip, Peter and I searched for Qala. We didn't know it was Maniilaq's birthplace, or even who Maniilaq was. We just saw the spot marked on our maps, indicating an abandoned Eskimo settlement. But there was nothing there to see. All we found were clouds of mosquitoes, brush, moose tracks, and a few depressions that could have been old house pits.

I often pass by the spot where Maniilaq camped, just below the mouth of Tunnuuraq. It's the lower end of Alex Sheldon's dog yard now; the slope is littered with rusted cans, caribou bones, and plastic bags. Just uphill is a tiny shack—one of Ambler's sewage pumping stations, often in poor repair. At times the stench can be overpowering. Few people know that this was the place where perhaps the greatest of The People was last seen in the Kobuk valley. When I ask my junior high students what they know about Maniilaq, most smile and shrug.

Spring is late this year. Mark Cleveland has just died, and now, in late May, when the willows should be sprouting and the river rushing by, snow lies three feet deep behind my cabin. I stand with old Shield Downey, looking out over the frozen Kobuk, which shows no sign of wakening. "When do you think it will break up?" I ask. "I don't know," he says. "Maybe this is the big winter that old man talked about."

*Never get caught out in the barren country
when it is cold and when it starts to get stormy.
Try to protect yourself and try to get to a place
where there is brush, and stay there until you are
sure that you can make it home. Take no
chances. Never stop at a place where there is a
snow bank which might get so big that you get
trapped in it. Sometimes carelessness ends up in
unbearable suffering.*

*. . . It has been said from generation to
generation that when a person starts to get
frozen and is beginning to get unconscious, he
feels that he is putting on a nice new jack rabbit
parka, and is starting to get warm. But that is
really the end of him.*

—James Wells, *Ipani Eskimos*

A Trip to the Store

△△△△△△△△△

Ready to go?" My friend Clarence Wood stands in the cabin doorway, rifle slung over his shoulder. The cold rolls in along the floor like smoke; outside, his snowmobile idles, hitched to a packed sled. I glance at the thermometer. Twenty below.

"Five minutes," I say. "Maybe ten."

"Well, I'll meet you on the trail. I'll take my time."

Fifteen minutes later I'm pounding along on my snowmobile, loaded sled fishtailing as I slam over rock-hard drifts in the darkness. My headlight casts a cone of wavering light before me, barely enough to steer by. Clumps of scrub willow loom like ghosts and blur past. The landscape, immense by daylight, seems as infinite and nebulous as the canyons of Pluto. I can't help wondering what the hell I'm doing here. I'm only five miles from town, and navigation has become an act of faith.

To Clarence, "taking my time" means twenty-five miles an hour over rough trail. It also means I have to do at least thirty to catch up. I duck low behind the windshield, squeeze the throttle, and try to ignore the pinprick tingles that tell me my nose is already freezing. I'm outfitted in full cold-weather gear: an inner suit of expedition-weight polypropylene, then pants and jacket of acrylic fleece, a shell jacket, a parka over that, and an enormous, foam-insulated coverall bib. My feet are sheathed in army surplus vapor-barrier boots—huge white clunkers that weigh two pounds apiece and are often called bunny boots for obvious reasons. My hands and head are my nod to Eskimo technology—beaverskin gauntlets up to my elbows and a beaverskin cap snugged tight, plus face mask and goggles. I feel and look like the

Michelin tire man. And yet the tip of my nose is frozen solid for the tenth time this winter.

We're after caribou along the Selawik trail, a regular grocery run for many of the upper Kobuk people. A mild autumn has kept a few thousand animals further north than usual, at the edge of the wide tundra flats thirty miles southeast of Ambler. The day before, Clarence had flashed his narrow-eyed smile and measured an inch between thumb and forefinger. "The cows with small horns are this faaat!" He drew the last word out, showing his teeth.

The Selawik trail is one of a web of winter routes stretching between the region's ten villages. Loosely marked by wooden tripods and stakes—sometimes a quarter-mile apart—the trail winds eighty miles to the southwest, around the southern flank of the Waring Mountains, across the Kuugruaq River, and down the windswept, treeless expanse of the Selawik valley to the village of the same name. Except for a shelter cabin at the halfway point, there are no improvements. The tripods are no more than reference points, reassurance that you're headed in the right direction. A little snow or wind, and the trail itself—no more than a ribbon of packed snow several yards wide—vanishes. Even in clear weather, it's possible for an experienced traveler to get good and lost. There are two or three such trails leading out of each village, less than two dozen in the entire region. This ephemeral network is the closest thing in the northwest arctic to a highway system; maintenance of the trails, in fact, is funded by the Alaska Department of Transportation. Travel on any of them is considered safe except in storms or severe cold, which isn't to say the journey will be easy or comfortable. Travelers are offered one very real consolation: if someone—anyone—is overdue, volunteer search-and-rescue teams from the closest village will set out in any weather, at any time of day, and search as long as it takes. Clarence is a veteran of many such searches, some of which have lasted for weeks, even months, long after everyone knows there's no hope.

Following the fresh grooves left by Clarence's sled, I crest a low tundra ridge and veer east off the main trail toward the Rabbit Mountains, a cluster of rounded peaks rising like an island from the flats. Camp is another few miles ahead, in the wide, rolling country near the range's southern flank—a place of wooded knolls, tundra, brushy creekbeds, and dozens of tiny frozen lakes that all look the same.

It's nearly 10:00 A.M., and the darkness is just now fading into a flat, cold gray, just enough to steer by. Full dawn is still a week distant; a December day in the arctic means five hours of pale light shrouded in ice fog. At noon, the sun hovers just below the horizon, casting a reddish glow over the land. By four, night settles in again.

I catch up at last, and Clarence leads me down a slope into a wooded basin, where he pitched a canvas wall tent the week before. Nestled in a stand of spruce against a kettle lake, it's protected from prevailing winds, and there's plenty of dry wood nearby. We fill the sheet metal woodstove, and as I coax a fire to life, my fingers stiffen.

Waiting for the sky to lighten enough for hunting, we drink coffee and talk of animals and machinery—two endless, interwoven topics that always seem to dominate our conversation. Though it's been scarcely a generation since the first snowmobiles came to the upper Kobuk, the *Ivisaappaamiut* have adopted them so completely that it's almost impossible to imagine what life was like four decades ago. Back then, at fourteen, Clarence did what most young men did—raised a dog team and began traveling the country. He would carry a gun, a few shells, a canvas tarp, some coffee, sugar and salt. Meat and fat came from the land, and so did his lessons.

But a quarter-century ago, Clarence got his first snowmobile. He and thousands of Inupiat made the transition as naturally as if these machines had one day sprouted out of the tundra, a new gift to be gathered and used, like a good chunk of jade or a fat caribou bull. Clarence ditched his dogs and learned the way of bearings, pistons, and of the cash economy that produced them. Jobs—construction, fire fighting, anything—became part of the subsistence cycle. But after a few weeks or months of working for pay, or, rather, for the machines that money would buy, he always returned to the world he knew, to the land that had made him.

But the need for meat remains the same. I ask Clarence how many caribou he gets a year. "I don't know," he says in his quiet, breathy voice. "Better than twenty-five, anyway. My grandchildren always want that fresh meat. Guess I spoil them."

A half-hour later we set out on our machines, angling through the open country along the blue-white curve of the Rabbit Mountains. From a distance, they'd seemed flat, two-dimensional; now, they're a maze of wooded slopes and small, steep valleys. We make our own trail, alternately leaning, standing, and kneeling as we ride, dodging trees, vaulting gullies, getting stuck now and then. Clarence is dragging his empty basket sled, hoping to fill it with carcasses. Since I've left mine in camp, I take the lead, breaking trail.

Caribou tracks are everywhere, the snow beaten into winding trails two feet wide and deep, torn down to bare ground in places. But there's nothing fresh, and no sign of the big herd that was here just a few days before. Then I catch a flash of movement—a half-dozen pale gray shapes trotting along the ridge 300 yards off. Clarence squints for a moment and shakes his head. "Bulls," he says. "Too skinny this time of year." I wonder how he knows, at this range, what sex they are. By now the bulls have shed their huge racks, lost a third of their body weight during the rutting frenzy, and look much the same as cows. "Only bulls? Are you sure?" I ask. Clarence cocks an eyebrow, wondering, no doubt, if I'm blind or just feebleminded. I don't ask again.

We ride over the crest of a ridge, and down through an old burn where the snow lies four feet deep. The powder sprays around my chest as I drive, kneeling on the seat, picking a route downhill through the charred stumps. Suddenly I realize that Clarence is no longer behind me. I loop back, and find him stalled out. "Ice in the fuel pump," he says, and pulls out a screwdriver. As he works barehanded, fingers soaked with subzero gasoline, I shudder. He finishes up and gives the starter rope a pull. The engine rattles, backfires, and dies. "Carburetor maybe," Clarence murmurs, and sets to work. Finally we build a fire to thaw it out, and the machine roars to life.

"Should we go back?" I ask.

"Caribou around here somewhere. Might as well keep heading this way," he says.

Weaving east along a steep-sided, brushy little creek for several miles, we scan the open tundra on either side of us. There are a few caribou trails, most of them stale. I stop to pull on my heavy mitts, and realize Clarence is missing again.

He's a half-mile back, tinkering under the hood. "Could be spark plugs," he says. My pocket thermometer reads thirty-four below zero, and the light is fading. We finally coax the engine to run, but only on one cylinder. Our hunt is over. Fresh meat will have to wait for another day.

The shortest way to camp now is to continue our loop around the mountain and then circle back. I ride slowly, breaking trail uphill for Clarence's laboring machine. Every quarter mile he bogs down or stalls. My left foot is numb, and I can feel the cold seeping through every seam.

At last his snowmobile can't even move on its own. "Piston, I guess. Or something." We still have at least five miles of rough tundra and gullies before us. We can either abandon his machine and ride double, or try to drag it back. We decide to save ourselves an extra trip if we can. Clarence fashions a towing yoke from sled rope, looped through his skis and tied to my hitch. He'll steer his machine, and it's up to me to break trail and navigate on the move. If I let up on the throttle at the wrong place—the bottom of a creek, say—we'll be hopelessly stuck. If I push my machine too hard and break something, we'll be walking.

We slam along, steering southwest, trying to avoid the deeper creekbeds. My engine screams under the strain, and I find myself sweating as I lean into a sidehill, fighting to keep the skis level. Brush slashes at my face. I look back, and Clarence waves directions. He knows the country so well that each creek or knoll is a street sign guiding us home.

Darkness has closed in by the time we reach the tent. I scramble inside to start the stove, anxious to thaw out my face. Clarence pulls off his gloves and works on his engine, a flashlight clamped in his teeth. Finally he comes inside, shaking his head in disgust. "Don't know. In the morning, maybe." He shows me where his wrist has been branded by cold metal.

We eat canned beans and pilot bread, stripping off parkas and coveralls as the stove glows red. Then, after coffee, we unroll our sleeping bags and bring in more wood. It's now forty-five below, and the air is so dense it seems liquid. A deep breath brings on a coughing spell.

I stoke the stove one last time, and nestle into my double bags, pulling the drawstring tight over my head.

"Goodnight, Clarence," I say.

"I tell you what," he mutters. "Pain in the ass traveling in the country today."

We have lived here as long as anyone can remember. Now it seems that the white man is trying to control everything. Although the people of this land have not really done anything wrong, once the white men allotted some land to the Inupiat, they tried to set up regulations which would let them keep control.

> —from the narrative of
> Joe Immaluuraq Sun, in *Lore of the Inupiat*

A person needs to be alert especially when it is a question of fine print such as you find in contracts because government workers are not alike. Some white men are smooth talkers and say they can do this or that or even go as far as saying they are the law, but they are only doing a job for money. You need to make sure what is expected of you on paper and make sure what your compensation will be. Take note. Be real sure.

> —from the narrative of
> Lawrence Akisaqpak Gray, in
> *Lore of the Inupiat*

Housekeeping in the
Northwest Arctic

△△△△△△△△△

J ust below the Noatak Canyon, where the Kuugruaq comes
in, there is a deep green pool, and just then—first week of
August, 1982—that pool was full of fish. Hundreds of them.
I was hoping for arctic char, but so far I hadn't been able to get my
spoon past the salmon. They were chums: hook-jawed males wide as a
thigh, eight to twelve pounds, the streamlined females smaller, all in
their mottled spawning colors. They were swirling all over the pool.
Now and then one erupted from the water and went bouncing along
like an outsized skipping stone before falling back with a wet crash.
Every fifth cast I was on to one, the rod bent hard, the drag buzzing.

What the salmon lacked in common sense, they made up with
teeth. I was cursing another lost spoon when I heard a boat whining
down the main river. This far above Noatak village—fifty miles—and
this early in August, outboards aren't common. It's too early for the
boatloads of caribou hunters from Kotzebue and Noatak; right now,
they're still down at the coast, commercial fishing or hunting seals.
If you see anyone, it's usually floaters, as the *Napaaqtugmiut* call them:
people from far away who have paid big money to kayak or canoe
down the Noatak from near the headwaters, some two or three hundred miles. Each year they come from all over the world to see what's
been called the largest unspoiled river valley in the United States: the
Noatak National Preserve.

The boat was close enough now that I could see it wasn't an
Eskimo at the tiller. I could hear it, too, the way his prop chewed
gravel as he took the wrong channel past the island. He was coming in
to land, standard river etiquette. If you run into someone out here,
stranger or no, it's a good excuse to take a break—trade information,

drink some coffee. I put down my rod and walked over to help him land. The driver was a small, wiry guy with a nervous red beard and a khaki uniform shirt. Not a game warden, or a state biologist, either; I knew the two stationed in Kotzebue, and Fred, who came from Fairbanks to study char every year.

"How they bitin'?" A southerner.

"Not bad. Only salmon, though."

"Yeah, I wet a line last night, and they sure were hungry."

"Well, chums don't eat in fresh water, do they? Strike out of instinct, or to protect their nests."

"Is that so. Can I see your license?"

"You could if I had it along. You're not a warden, are you? I know Rolin."

"Walt Shipman, National Park Service. I'm the ranger for this stretch of the preserve." I shook hands and squinted at the patch on his sleeve.

"Well, Walt, it's not on me. You can check on it with Rolin, though. He knows I've got one." Not even the start of a smile—just the red beard twitching. The guy was serious.

"You should have it in your possession at all times."

"Yeah, but there's never a warden around up here at this time of year. He's at the coast, checking salmon permits."

"I'm here." Loaded .357 on his hip and all.

"Well, I've been around a while, and you're my first ranger."

"Not the last. We're building a station down by the Kelly, another up by the Cutler. This is federal land, and we're here to protect it."

"How long you been up here?"

"Six weeks."

"Where you from?"

"Tennessee."

"Well, good luck to you."

"Same to you. Say, you know whose wall tent that is up the bar?"

"Mine."

"Can I see your permit?"

"Permit? Since when?"

"Since now. If you don't have one, it'll have to come down."

"Just a minute. That tent has been there over a year. The state people know it, and it's never been a problem. I keep the area clean. Anyone can use it."

"This ain't state land. It's a national preserve. But I'll give you some time to get your permit."

"Where do I get one? From you?"

"Nope. You gotta talk to the main office in Kotzebue. Excuse me, I have to check up on these folks." A couple of double kayaks had come around the bend, drifting quietly with the current. Walt shoved off and roared out. When he cut his motor to talk, I heard his voice carry over the water.

"How you folks doin'? Walt Shipman, National Park Service . . ."

The Noatak National Preserve was officially born in December 1980, when Jimmy Carter signed into law the Alaska National Interest Lands Conservation Act (better known as "d-2" because it was first presented under Section 17 (d) (2) of the Alaska Native Claims Settlement Act, the monumental piece of legislation that stemmed from the discovery of oil at Prudhoe Bay). As a result, the National Park Service gained thirteen new pieces of land to administer, all in Alaska, all varying shades of huge. The big question was how. These monuments, as they were classified for the time being, were different from any parklands in the Lower 48; for one thing, almost none of them had road access. The single biggest chunk—the 16 million acres of the abutting Kobuk, Gates of the Arctic, and Noatak monuments—was completely above the arctic circle and remote in the fullest sense, grazed only in the eastern corner by the pipeline haul road. It included a god-sized handful of river valleys, and much of the central and western Brooks Range. There it was, park service land. Now, what to do with it?

It's not as if the park service had been taken by surprise; under the 1958 Statehood Act, the federal government had the right to select a little Alaskan land for itself. All told, it ended up with 131 million acres, to be divided among its four conservation systems: the National Park, Forest, Wildlife Refuge, and Wild and Scenic Rivers. The park service knew all along they'd be getting theirs, and they had some ideas of what they wanted. However, not until the Alaska Native Claims Settlement Act became law in 1971 could the actual selection process move forward. Studies started in 1972, culminating in House Bill HR 39, introduced by Morris Udall in 1977. The bill made it through the House, but died in the Senate. In late 1978, as the time limit set by the Native Claims Act was almost up, Interior Secretary Cecil Andrus withdrew 140 million acres under emergency authority given him by the Federal Land Policy and Management Act of 1976. Using the Antiquities Act of 1906 for a loophole, Jimmy Carter immediately signed public proclamations that earmarked 56 million acres as national monuments. Nothing was settled, though the land was safely tied up—temporarily. The stopgap measure worked; in August of 1980 a compromise version of HR 39 finally passed the Senate and was on the president's desk by December.

By that time, the park service had already been working for nearly two years to establish themselves as suzerains of the new monuments; Carter's proclamations had all but promised those thirteen huge parcels to them. They'd done nothing overt to the land itself; what they had done was to take inventory, show the colors a bit, and start putting together a set of rules. That was plenty to keep them busy.

The land had always been there, restricted by few regulations and fewer boundaries. Alaska residents, Native and white, were used to doing pretty much whatever they wanted, wherever and whenever: kill a moose, build a cabin, stake a mining claim. That was the way it had always been. The pipeline's coming and the Native Claims Act may have marked the de facto end of that wide freedom, but nothing much had really happened far out in the bush; the land was still there, and there was still so little enforcement that you could usually ignore the invisible things called rules.

Then The Feds came. They told people to get out of unauthorized cabins on monument land, told sport hunters and guides they couldn't hunt there anymore, told prospectors they had to leave. They passed out booklets from Anchorage to Anaktuvuk Pass, called public meetings to explain endless pages of fine print with menacing titles: Federal Register, Department of the Interior, National Parks Service: Alaska National Monuments; General Management Regulations: Part I. A few months later came Part II. Rural Alaskans were understandably divided in their reactions to The Feds—they either disliked them or outright hated them. Explaining good intentions was no use. Nobody wanted to hear the official line that these lands were entrusted to the park service so that they could be passed on "in unimpaired condition to future generations" while still "providing for use and enjoyment." The irony was the park service's conscious desire to establish a hands-off management style resulted in so many restrictions for local residents. The park service people and their booklets were the first tangible symbols of the new order, the first actual targets for rebellion. All considered, it's remarkable most of those meetings went as smoothly as they did.

I was at the monument regulations meeting in Ambler, on September 6, 1979. Maybe twenty of the village's fifty-odd adults sat in undersized elementary school chairs and listened to what The Feds had to say. Most of the listeners were Inupiat: Robert Cleveland, the mayor; Clarence Wood, Nelson and Edna Greist, Merill Morena—the only Eskimo under forty was Frank Downey. The young men of the village were somewhere else. A few of Ambler's small white community turned out: Dave Rue, owner and operator of Ambler Air; Dan Denslow, retired pilot and bush renaissance man; Pete MacManus, veteran teacher and Iditarod dog musher; Erik VanVeenen, hunting guide and owner of Ambler Trading. As his flunky, I sat next to him. Facing us from behind a table were The Feds: Mack Shaver, the new Superintendent of Monuments in the region, and Ray Bane, a dog mushing cultural anthropologist with nineteen years of bush experience. Side by side, the two were a study in contrast—Mack, with his neatly pressed uniform shirt and every hair apparently glued in place, an incarnation of Dudley Do-Right; Ray, a bearded, balding, spectacled, muscular gnome of a man, in worn sweater and jeans. What linked them was emotion. Both were visibly nervous, and had the careworn air of men who knew they should be.

With Mack and Ray were two representatives from NANA, the Northwest Arctic Native Association. One was Robert Newlin, a small man with the benign aspect and the round belly of a Chinese Buddha—and a wristwatch that flashed with gold nuggets and jade from across the room. Robert was there to translate the park service's complex spiel into Inupiaq, and to provide a reassuring presence, the stamp of NANA's approval. The other NANA representative was a much younger Eskimo, maybe in his late twenties—a representative of the first Inupiat generation to speak English as a preferred language; one of those raised in a world of snow machines and daily jet flights into Kotzebue, though he would surely not describe himself in such terms.

The meeting had two purposes: to explain the latest metamorphosis of the monument regulations (Part II, just now); and to solicit comments and suggestions from the people who had called this country home for thousands of years. With Robert slowly translating, Mack Shaver and Ray Bane assured the people of Ambler that their input was important, and that it could well be a factor in shaping park service policy.

"We are here as housekeepers, not house builders."

"We want to protect the traditional Eskimo way of life, and we need your advice to do this."

Everyone listened as The Feds explained that local subsistence use of monument resources had priority over all other human activities. The people of Ambler could continue to hunt, fish, trap, cut wood, and gather plants in the monument areas that surrounded them. Recreational use by hikers, boaters, and fishermen from the Outside would be allowed, with conditions. Any area of the monuments could be temporarily or permanently closed to recreational use if such use interfered with local subsistence. For instance, when the fall caribou migration comes pouring through Onion Portage, just below Ambler, hikers might be restricted from the area if they were interfering in any way with traditional hunting. Sport hunting, mining, and other commercial ventures would be banned.

"Yeah, we'll keep all white people off our land forever!" The young NANA man suddenly launched into a tirade, and everyone, white and Eskimo, just sat and said nothing. Ray tactfully moved to another topic, hinting that this vision was not exactly what the park service had in mind. But from time to time, the man burst out with his opinions, though no one encouraged him. On the other hand, no one encouraged The Feds either. Most of the audience discussion so far had been in Inupiaq, with minimal translation offered by Robert. Neither the park service men nor the white residents of Ambler knew exactly what was being said. By watching faces and listening for tone of voice, though, you could tell that most of the *Ivisaappaatmiut* were more bemused than anything else. Why all the fuss? The land looked the same as always, and the past two years the caribou had been thicker than ever. There had been no flood of *naluaqmiut.* Who was that big game warden, anyway?

The villagers looked at maps as Ray and Mack explained recreational access plans for Kobuk Monument. Hikers could be dropped by floatplanes at this big lake, here, far enough from Ambler and the Kobuk River so that no one would be bothered. The discussion suddenly became more animated after Ray pointed to the place labeled "Caribou Lake." After a long confabulation in Inupiaq, marked by lengthy pauses, Tommy Lee, one of the patriarchs of Ambler, addressed the visitors, his voice tactful but firm.

"That place we always call *Isaakaaqlik*. That means place where ducks and geese stay when they can't fly. We hunt there early summertime. Not a good place for planes, maybe. Too much bother those birds." This was the only amendment to the plan suggested that night. And so the monument map was changed to read Isaakaaqlik Lake instead, and the park service had to find another access point.

In the back of the room, Erik had been muttering to himself for the past half hour. Half of his guiding territory was now inside the monuments. He'd known that for a year, but had pretty much gone on with business as usual. There hadn't been any park service enforcement so far, and the state wardens, who had reasons of their own not to love The Feds, were interested only in compliance with state laws. And Erik's mostly German clientele, who paid up to $10,000 for a two-week hunt, were interested only in results. So what if some of the best grizzly and sheep country in the state was on the wrong side of the new boundaries? The Feds were off in Washington someplace, counting paper clips and looking at maps.

Now, though, the National Park Service was a uniformed, immaculately groomed reality—right here in Ambler. Erik's internal pot boiled over. He stood and addressed The Feds, his cold, measured vehemence more commanding than any shout.

"Nazis, that's what you are. A pack of Nazis! You can fool these people, but you don't fool me." He turned to the Eskimo audience. "You're playing into their hands, every one of you. You think you're being smart, that they're going to protect everything for you, but just wait—you'll all be regulated out of subsistence. Bit by bit, so you hardly notice. Then they'll take over and that's it."

No one reacted directly, though some eyes shifted to the floor in puzzled embarrassment. Not even the young NANA hotshot knew what to say. I sat there, wishing I could click my heels three times and end up in Kansas. Ray Bane cleared his throat. He'd known Erik for years, not always on an unfriendly basis. "Now just a minute, Erik. . . ."

"You, Ray, you've lived here long enough to know the truth. Why don't you tell these people that The Feds are here to take away their land? You're one of us, whoring himself out."

"I don't consider myself a whore, and we are not here to take away anything. We are going to have roads up here, we are going to have mines. Like it or not, it's all coming, and there's no way to stop it. We have to protect the land where we can, and the park service is doing its best." Ray spoke in measured, clear tones, his face flushed. It wouldn't do to get into a shouting match—not with his boss, NANA representatives, and a roomful of *Ivisaappaatmiut* watching.

"Go ahead, make your noise. We'll do what we want, just as we always have."

"You will not."

"Do you really think any of these people care about your rules or your parks? You think they're going to send in written suggestions? They didn't ask for you to save them."

"Erik . . ."

"I'm done. Go to hell and take your little books with you."

That was 1979. The National Park Service has been in northwest arctic Alaska for ten years now. On the Noatak, rangers come and go—they rotate in from Outside, stay a year, perhaps two, and move on; but the station above the Kelly River is a fixture, a place for travelers to sometimes stop and have coffee. It's open during the short open-water season, June through September. The station at the Cutler, though, another 150 miles upstream, has been shut down. There's one ranger living on the edge of 6.5 million acres of land. No campsites have been built, no signs posted; the patrols are infrequent, limited almost always to the main river. There are other park service personnel around now and then: field biologists studying caribou or Dall sheep, or some of the Kotzebue office people out on patrol. The Noatak country rolls to the horizon—mountains and valleys, more mountains and valleys, almost the same as it was before the park service, almost the same as it was before the first missionaries and miners came.

Almost. In June, as soon as spring breakup is done, the first floaters of the season come drifting down the Noatak. Most charter a floatplane to the headwaters for $500 to $1,000, and paddle the 300 miles to Noatak village. Some hire guides or travel in groups, some go

it alone. They catch grayling, take pictures, watch gyrfalcons and caribou, and set up their bright nylon tents on gravel bars where wandering hunters camped a thousand years before. Some take hikes off the
main river and back into the hills, but not many go far. A few miles of
wet tundra, brush, and unstable slopes strained through a cloud of
mosquitoes is usually enough. Beyond the main river and the first line
of hills, there are mountains that have probably never been climbed,
valleys where only Eskimo trappers have been.

But every year there are more floaters, and from further and further away—Japanese and Texans, Germans and New Yorkers. In
1986, more than a hundred parties came down the river, and the numbers are steadily climbing. A hundred parties—fewer than a thousand
people—may not seem like many, but considering that by the mid-
1970s only a handful of outsiders had made the trip, the increase has
been astronomical. The pressure can only build as word spreads.

Ironically, the adventurers have been attracted by those who most
wanted to keep the land as remote wilderness. Two *National Geographic* articles in the '70s first brought the Noatak to international
attention; in tones smacking slightly of myth, the first story described a
joint *National Geographic*/National Park Service expedition, one of
those early inventory-taking trips when the service was looking at what
they wanted. There was much sermonizing about preserving the valley
in its pristine state. The second article, written by park service officer
John Kauffmann in 1977, was timed perfectly to reinforce the first.
For thousands of readers, the vivid photography and descriptions gave
shape to imagination. Daydreams of Alaska now had a specific destination: in Kauffmann's words, "an entire mountain-ringed wilderness
basin, the last of its kind and magnitude in the United States." I was
one of those dreamers, and it was no accident that when I finally
moved from dreams into action, I headed straight for the Noatak. And
it was no accident that two years later, after starting off in Ambler, I
found a job as a teacher in Noatak village and moved there.

Besides the *Geographic* stories, there are the handsome glossy
brochures from the park service, the guide books, and the beckoning
colored park boundaries on dozens of maps. The Noatak Valley. The
biggest and most remote chunk of park service land—the trip of a
lifetime. The dreamers come from everywhere, each carrying his
or her own visions north to match against the shimmering expanse of

land. Some are disappointed to find tents around the bend, footprints on gravel bars in what should be the far edge of nowhere.

Floaters and hikers are only one of three groups who use the valley, and they probably have the smallest impact. They catch a few fish and quietly paddle on. Then there are Caucasian sportsmen and Inupiat subsistence hunter-gatherers competing in ever-increasing numbers, equipped with the increasingly sophisticated toys of modern technology: STOL (short takeoff and landing) aircraft that can use any scrap of reasonably level ground; boats with huge outboards; hundred mile-an-hour snowmobiles; semiautomatic carbines. The whole valley is open to the traditional subsistence users, but the sport hunters have to stay south of the Cutler River, in what is now the Noatak Preserve. The preserve designation allows for broader use than do the monument or park labels. Broader use includes sport hunting. Guides like Erik, the National Rifle Association, and prohunting private citizens had a strong enough lobbying voice to make the park service listen, and it was decided that Alaska was unique enough and large enough to accommodate everyone.

The sport hunters got roughly 7 million acres, former monument areas redesignated as "preserves," including much of the Noatak valley. The preserve designation also allows mining and timber harvest, by permit. Upstream from the Cutler and south into the Kobuk drainage, though, are the Gates of the Arctic and Kobuk Valley national parks around Ambler—9 million prime acres where sport hunting and commercial development are strictly prohibited.

On paper, anyway. The region's only state game warden got transferred south in 1986 without a replacement—budget cuts—and the already overloaded Alaska state troopers were forced to handle game enforcement until a warden was reassigned a year later. He can't keep up with hit-and-run airplane hunters any more than the park service can. As one airplane hunter smugly put it, "Hell—we're weasels in the henhouse and the dog's nowhere around."

Needless to say, there is no love lost between the sport hunters and the Native subsistence users. The former covet the latter's rights to hunt inside the parks, and more:

"Those friggers live like kings. Subsistence, hah. No more than me. They get government checks and food stamps and shoot ten caribou just for the tongues."

"Murderous bastards. Those Natives kill whatever they want, when they want, and no one stops them." So says one hunting guide known for his unscrupulous use of aircraft.

On the other side, the Inupiat claim—probably with good cause—that all the airplane traffic along the main river scares the animals back into the hills, where they are far harder to hunt and nearly impossible to pack out in the needed numbers. Stories circulate among the villagers:

"Lots of caribous walking down the mountain, right for us, and then some plane come. It keep circling, chase all of them back."

"Those guides, they always take heads and leave meat."

And neither group cares much for the park service: "Even them park rangers. One time that boat come, right when we were going to shoot, and we never get nothing. That ranger know he chase them away, and he just smile."

"You got to hate those Feds. Screwed this whole country up for everybody."

Luckily for everyone, especially the park service, the floaters, sport hunters, and subsistence users don't cross paths too often. The floating season is June through August, when most Eskimos are down at the coast, commercial fishing and hunting belugas. September and early October is the big sport hunting time. For at least eight months of the year, the Inupiat have the valley more or less to themselves.

But there is one time when all three groups occupy the same space: Labor Day into the first week of September. The commercial fishing season is over, and the Noatak people return to the village. It's time for children to go back to school, for the women to pick berries and cut salmon for drying, and for the men to go hunting. They load a drum of gas or two into their big wooden boats, throw in wall tents and supplies for two weeks, and head upriver. Past the Kelly, the Noatak Canyons, the Poktovik Mountains, the Nakolik, the Nimiuktuq . . . some go as far as the Cutler, a full 200 miles above the village, nearly 300 miles from summer camp on the coast. It depends on where the caribou are. The *Napaaqtugmiut* set camp near one of the usual crossings and work out of there, hoping to catch a band on or near the river. If the hunters are lucky, they'll return to the village with their boat wallowing beneath the weight of carcasses—ten or fifteen caribou, and maybe a Dall sheep, moose, or a bear as well. Just now the village is hungry for the first fresh meat of the season, and everything will be eaten.

Right behind the Noatak hunters come the Kotzebue people. Most of them don't travel as far upriver, but there are more of them, with bigger, faster boats.

And overhead, everywhere, are the airplanes: Cessnas, Supercubs, Citabrias, and Maules carrying sport hunters from all over Alaska, the U.S., and the world. An old joke calls mosquitoes the Alaska state bird, and these act and sound the part—mosquitoes out of a nightmare. Many of the pilots fly right on the deck, right up the main river and up the side valleys at altitudes as low as a hundred feet. Flying and hunting on the same day is illegal, cause for forfeiting your plane, but what if a bear shows up near a good gravel bar, no ranger in sight? There is a law forbidding low flying in certain corridors, but it's seldom enforced.

Drifting haplessly down into this fierce mechanical circus come the last floaters of the season. Until past the Cutler, most have been lucky to see only a few others of their kind. Suddenly there are hunting camps every five bends, and the infernal aircraft whining overhead. A small group of kayakers from Des Moines might be watching a band of caribou ford the river when a powerboat full of Eskimos comes roaring in. As the floaters watch in horror, a dozen bulls are wiped out in a point-blank barrage. The Inupiat wave as they retrieve floating carcasses and drag them to shore. Maybe they pull up and ask the floaters to join them for coffee, and offer some good fresh meat.

The weather turns cold, and by the third week of September, the slush ice is flowing. The weather goes sour—snow, wind, rain, and fog; only the professional guides are flying. The ranger station at the Kelly closes down, and the Noatak valley quietly slides into the long, dark winter, as it has for centuries.

Until next year.

One winter night I was beginning to be restless again, and I was going from mountain to mountain when I noticed a little bright light not very far away. I went to see what it was, and when I came upon it there was an ivrulik *[sod house—here, a metaphor for a womb] with a very bright light in it. My desire to enter was so great I had no fear of what should happen to me. After what seemed such a short time I was born with five* amagauyaat *(wolf cubs). Once more I became a wolf.*

. . . Seeing the mother that now reared us, she seemed no different from that other one in her interest for our welfare. I knew that this female wolf loved us all, and took care of us the very best she knew how. I had been a wolf two times now, and had no further desire to find a mother among humans.

—from "Nathlook: Susie, My Name," in Lela Kiana Oman's *Eskimo Legends*

The Circle of the Kill

⌃⌃⌃⌃⌃⌃⌃⌃⌃⌃

I was sixty miles from home when I saw the tracks—those of a lone moose, nothing special except that they were fresh, crisply etched in new snow, and headed in the same direction I was. Tired from five days of traveling with a heavy sled, I watched them disappear under my snowmobile's skis without paying much notice. I'd already come seventy miles, from the northern rim of the Noatak valley, across the Imelyak, and over the rolling high tundra of Amakomanaq—an umarked trail Clarence had shown me years ago. Ahead lay Ivishak Pass, a notorious wind tunnel, and I wanted to get through while the morning calm held.

Another set of tracks merged in from the left. Wolf. I slowed down, leaned forward, and started paying attention. The size of the prints meant a young adult or a big pup, and here and there the loping animal's paws blurred over the moose trail. Then other wolves joined in from the east, more tracks than I could sort out. The snow before me was trampled in a maze, and there was a mound of wolf scat. Probably a day or two old, I thought, and slowed down for a look. Where was the pack now? I skidded to a stop. The pile was steaming. For the first time in a quarter mile I looked up, and fifty yards away a wolf stood in the ice fog. Tail out, stiff legged, it regarded me, and our eyes met.

Something in the stare of a wolf is chilling, beyond the hungry yellow eyes of childhood nightmares, beyond any physical threat, real or imagined. Caught in that cold glare, I felt suddenly transparent, as if my heart were being measured. In that instant I knew what we fear most in wolves: not their teeth but their wisdom—an alien, elusive intelligence that refuses us, rejects our notions of superiority with a glance.

161

We faced each other, motionless in the half light, suspended in our surprise. I watched the pulsing steam of its breath, and realized I'd been holding mine. Then the wolf turned. Things began to move again. I followed its gaze to a nearby slope, and there were dark shapes in the brush, a dozen wolves standing together, looking down toward us, waiting for what would happen next. Ravens rose and circled, squawking. The wolf in my trail stepped toward me and stopped. The next move was mine.

In thirteen years of moving through wolf country, I've felt menaced only once, and that animal, young and inexperienced, probably meant no harm. Every wolf I've ever encountered—maybe four dozen in all that time—has either turned tail or ignored me. Here, riding a snowmobile and carrying a rifle, I knew there was no danger. In fact, I was surprised that the wolves had allowed themselves to be seen. Even in these remote mountains, most packs have learned that snowmobiles mean trouble—Eskimo wolf hunters, my friends among them. Why, then, was this wolf not only standing its ground, but approaching?

Maybe he was speaking to me. The wolf stepped toward me and stopped. I eased my idling machine forward an equal distance. The wolf repeated his question, and I answered again. There was surely no threat between us now, only curiosity, a desire to know. Forty yards apart, we studied each other. I don't know what the wolf saw. I remember a long-legged, thin, silver gray creature with a shabby coat and luminous eyes, head down, ears cocked, probing.

Then he was gone. In a blur I felt more than saw, the wolf pivoted and launched himself uphill. Ahead, the pack was in full flight, heads out, tails back, merging into single file as they burst up the slope, running hard for a windswept crag far above the valley floor. Pausing on the skyline, they took a last look and disappeared.

Halfway up the slope I found the kill. Entrails, bones, clumps of hair, and bloody snow were all that remained of the moose. Even the hide had been gnawed and swallowed, and bones cracked for their thread of marrow. The skull, still attached to the spine, had been polished clean. The story of the hunt was there in the snow: The cow had been trotting along the base of the ridge when the first wolf appeared behind her. She turned several times, harassed but not seriously threatened. Distracted, she sensed the ambush too late. The wolves charged downhill through the brush. She wheeled, but was driven back by the first wolf. The pack surrounded her and drew blood, slashing at flanks and hindquarters. More wolves arrived. While some rested, others pressed home the attack. The snow was trampled in circular patterns over several hundred yards, and at each place the cow had made a stand.

Finally, she floundered uphill into deep snow. The wolves pursued, and one slashed in, spilling open her belly. She struggled another thirty yards, dragging her intestines. The end came quickly as the pack mobbed her off her feet.

By the time I'd arrived, no more than three hours later, she had almost disappeared. Thirteen wolves had eaten over six hundred pounds of flesh—close to fifty pounds each. Nearby was a place where the pack had sat together, and I imagined them full-bellied, heads tilted back, singing of the hunt.

I spent more than an hour near the kill, circling as the wolves had done, reading their story in the snow, studying spots of blood, bits of hair. The intertwined trails seemed graceful, as if the wolves and moose had danced together. At the end of their dance lay the kill, beautiful in its simplicity. Here on this silent white hillside, there was no horror. This was their life—an endless hunt, an endless celebration of death.

As I stood within the circle of the kill, looking down at wolf prints frozen in blood, I brushed against their secret: wolves understand death perfectly. That's the bright, cold wisdom we see in their eyes, the thing that makes us afraid. Death is their art, their beauty, while it's our darkness and terror. If we ever understood what they know, we've forgotten. Maybe we're drawn to them because they remember.

It got toward spring. Autuyuk started walking upriver to look for his wife, to see if she had lived. The weather was nice and he stopped anywhere when he got tired. He walked along the west side of the river. When he got somewhere around the Kelly River he saw somebody sitting under a tree leaning against it. It was his wife.

He got real close and saw the upper half of a body hanging from a branch in the tree. He sat down and told his wife, "You still live. Let's go home from here." She said, "No, I am not fit for that anymore now." He wanted to take her, but she didn't want to go. He asked, "Where are your parents, your sisters, and brother?" She answered: "They all starved except for my brother. He is still alive. He took a knife and tried to kill me for food. That half body up there is one of my parents. I took it along for food when I ran from my brother."

—from the autobiography of
Edna Hunnicutt, *The Eskimo Storyteller*,
by Edwin S. Hall, Jr.

A Good Thing

▲▲▲▲▲▲▲▲▲

Looking at Nelson Greist, it's hard to imagine that he once nearly starved to death. Claiming that his girth equals his five and a half feet of height is an exaggeration—barely—and yet he wears his corpulence well; there is tremendous strength implied in the thick legs and arms. Walking down the dirt streets of Ambler, he moves with a measured dignity, the economical grace of a whale. His broad, dark face is so engaging that your eyes unconsciously dwell on it as he speaks. His features are classic full-blooded Inupiat Eskimo: full-lipped, generous mouth; wide cheekbones and prominent brow framing dark Mongolian eyes, delicately upswept at the corners; high forehead sloping into thick iron-gray hair. Somehow Nelson would not look out of place in a banker's pinstripes, though in all probability he's never worn a tie. He just has the presence to pull it off.

His people came from the North Slope, not far from Barrow. They were subsistence nomads, living in tents in summer, moving into sunken sod houses framed with whale ribs and drift timber for the long winter. They moved as resources dictated, hunting sea mammals on the spring ice, shifting inland for waterfowl, then stalking caribou as the herds returned to their summer calving grounds. They gathered most of their needs from the land and bartered for the rest at trading centers like Barrow. Nelson remembers hunting ptarmigan with bow and arrow as a boy.

"Gonna hard live that way, moving, always hunt, hunt, hunt. We always thinking if we gonna eating."

In the mid-1950s, Nelson's father decided to move his family south to the relatively benign climate of the upper Kobuk River, the land of the *Kuuvangmiit* (upper Kobuk) Eskimos. There was wood here for building and warmth; access to the caribou migrations; salmon, sheefish, and whitefish runs in the river. Also, there were villages here with small trading posts, churches, and schools. Nelson's father knew a good thing when he saw it. One day in early spring the family packed what they could carry and headed south.

It was the traditional time for cross-country travel: the sun was climbing higher every day, bringing warmer temperatures and long days. The snow in most places was packed firm by wind and cold, making for good trail. The Greists would cover about 350 miles of uninhabited country, climbing the windswept open tundra of the North Slope, crossing the continental divide into the upper Noatak valley at Anaktuvuk Pass, and threading through the Schwatka Mountains into the Kobuk drainage via Natmaktugiaq Pass. Once through the pass, it was a paltry seventy miles down the Ambler to the main river.

They nearly starved on the way. Spring was not only the traditional season for travel, but also for famine, especially as the trail softened in the latter part of April and early May. Frozen rivers became treacherous and drifts bottomless, sapping energy and slowing the pace. The land seemed empty, the caribou not yet returned from their wintering grounds south of the Kobuk. The food carried was nearly gone.

"Gonna sometimes we get up in nighttime and start travel. Can't sleep, no food. We thinking maybe gonna caribou somewhere."

Already weakened, Nelson's father fell seriously ill and died. Somewhere in the trackless mountains north of the Noatak, they left him in a makeshift grave and traveled on. Eventually the Greists struggled into the village of Shungnak and settled there, just as their father had planned.

Nelson met a local woman, married, and moved to the new village of Ambler, twenty-five miles west of Shungnak. Nelson and Edna Greist built a small log cabin on the bluff overlooking the Kobuk and began raising a family. Although he had arrived in the Kobuk valley almost destitute, Nelson was a hard worker, an able hunter, and a fine trapper. Cash for trade goods came from the beaver, fox, wolf, and lynx he caught, and the land provided meat, fish, berries, and building supplies. Edna sewed winter clothing from caribou skins and furs and bore many children.

But Nelson could not forget his father. Many times over the following years, he and his brother tried to retrace their steps and bring the remains home, but the grave was small and the country vast. He was finally forced to give up the search.

Nelson was now a successful commercial fisherman, working the late summer chum salmon run in Kotzebue. The family loaded a canvas wall tent and whatever else they needed into Nelson's big plywood riverboat and motored down the Kobuk 150 miles each June. They hunted seals and beluga on the Chukchi Sea until the salmon run began, and stored the precious oil and fat in wooden casks for winter. The salmon were gillnetted and sold to processors who flew the iced fish south to canneries and markets. When the chum season closed in late August, it was time to return to Ambler for caribou hunting, berry picking, fall whitefish, and school for the children. The cash from fishing—whatever it was—would last until next year.

Then, in the mid-'70s, Nelson saw the pipeline money flood into Ambler—the high school, airport, clinic, sewer system, satellite television, and all the rest. Prefabricated houses were made available through the federally funded Alaska State Housing Authority; for fifty dollars a month people could move into and eventually own identical frame dwellings with linoleum floors, galvanized roofs, water and sewer, and storm windows.

Nelson Greist knew a good thing when he saw it, and soon his old log house became a storage shed. He discovered with the rest of the *Ivisaappaatmiut* that the new houses were shoddily constructed and designed with Arizona rather than the arctic in mind. Pipes froze and snow filtered into the living room when the wind was fierce. Still, it was progress, and nearly free—except for the electricity and phone bills, and the water bills which were ignored once the million-dollar system froze solid. The new oil furnace proved impossibly expensive, and Nelson returned to burning wood. Eventually a thousand dollar wood heater was installed free of charge, and insulation added. Everybody got a new stove just by signing on a line. The money was there.

Nonetheless, the house required much more wood than his old cabin, which meant more trips on the snow machine, more gas, more repairs. Nelson found himself caught in a spiraling cash economy. The thought of trapping beaver to cover flour, sugar, salt, calico, and bullets was suddenly ludicrous. He had journeyed so far into a land of paper money that a return was impossible.

"Everything gonna high price, all right. Sometimes always can't even pay store bills. Little box of grub, gonna fifty dollar."

Nelson enrolled in the federal food stamp program along with nearly everyone in town. Without food stamps people probably wouldn't starve, but neither could they afford the canned goods, eggs, pop, and cookies they had become accustomed to. Eskimo food—caribou, moose, frozen whitefish, muktuk, seal oil, berries—was still the core of their diet, but it was no longer enough.

Television's portrayal of the American dream played a huge role in redefining the Greist's world. The glossy ads and programs created wants of all sorts—culinary, material, perhaps even spiritual—where few had existed. Immaculately dressed, perfectly groomed Caucasians paraded endlessly through scenes of mind-boggling luxury.

"Gonna white people have everything. Rich people, I see for myself."

One of the many projects and programs directed at the upper Kobuk in the post-pipeline era was funded by Control Data Corporation. The idea was to establish a modest agricultural operation to explore the potential of arctic farming. Potatoes were selected for a pilot crop, due to their ability to resist frost and their generally hardy nature. Control Data sought energetic, adaptable locals to learn potato farming from the ground up. Nelson Greist was their man. He knew a good thing when he saw it.

The project required reasonable soil quality with minimal permafrost. Above the arctic circle, most of the land is permanently frozen somewhere below the surface; ice might start less than a foot down, or it might be four. The most certain way to find good ground is to look for healthy spruce growth, since their root systems need space and well-drained ground. The searchers found such a place four miles up the Ambler River on the east bank. There was good southerly exposure, and protection from cooling north winds was afforded by an adjoining wooded slope of Ingichuk Mountain.

What was more, this land was available. One of the ironies of life in northwest arctic Alaska regards the expanse of land—accessible to all, with no fences, signs, or irate landowners. But on paper, it all has assigned domain, if not outright ownership. On certain maps, the region, like the rest of the state, is carved up into a complex grid of color-coded boundaries: The National Park Service, Bureau of Land Management, State of Alaska, the NANA Regional Corporation, the various Native villages, individual Native land allotments, fragments of private land, and mining claims.

Hunting, traveling, trapping, camping, gathering, and so on would be acceptable use without permission; hacking down a stand of timber and growing potatoes certainly would not be. But the plot in question belonged to NANA. The corporation was anxious to establish Eskimos in various enterprises, anxious to assert regional autonomy wherever possible. Local agriculture, growing potatoes instead of importing them from outside, seemed a good idea. NANA gave Nelson and his backers the go-ahead.

A D6 Cat was barged in, and Nelson got a new heavy-duty chain saw on credit. A cat skinner was imported to get things moving and to instruct Nelson. They would clear and prepare for planting the following year.

Ripping down forty acres of sizeable timber, winching out stumps and rocks, and tilling the ground was more than a good summer's work, even with additional hired help. Nelson's salmon permit went unused. For the first year in ten, the Greist family spent the summer in Ambler. They got checks, but now they would have to buy or barter for seal oil and blubber. There was no time for subsistence. The crew worked up through freezeup in October and on and off through the winter, felling trees.

One still evening the following July, 1981, I was motoring down the Ambler, returning from a few hours of fishing at the mouth of Miluet Creek. As I neared Nelson's farm, I saw a smudge fire still burning at the entrance of his tent cabin. It was past midnight, but at this time of year it's normal for people to stay up all night. I pulled in to say hello, and Nelson's beaming face appeared before I hit the bank.

"Gonna coffee? We got hot water." There was Edna in her bright calico, a loose long-sleeved pullover worn over slacks. Her smile was as wide as Nelson's.

"You get lotsa graylings? *Aarigaa,* good!" They politely turned down my offer of fresh fish; they had a net in the eddy just above. Nelson walked me around the brown muddy clearing. Great brushpiles and heaped boulders marked the field's edge. Rows of straggling green plants showed something was going on underground, but they scarcely looked robust.

"Too much rain, gonna too cold this summer." Nelson shook his head. "Maybe not so big this time."

"Next year, Nelson. It takes time to get the ground ready."

"Oh, we gonna business, all right!" He smiled hugely. "Now coffee." The inside of the tent cabin was pleasantly cluttered. They had erected a ten-by-twelve canvas wall tent and reinforced the walls with plywood sheeting. Chunks of sod were banked against the outside, and a plastic tarp stretched on a spruce pole frame over the roof. With a wooden sleeping platform, shelving, and a woodstove fashioned from the bottom third of an oil drum, the structure was comfortable and effectively winterized. In conception it was not unlike the sod houses Nelson had been raised in.

We sat chatting as the evening deepened, and watched a vole scurry about from wall to wall, collecting crumbs. Outside a heavy dew was forming, just above the frost point. A few years ago, such a phenomenon would have meant little to Nelson in a practical sense, but now he peered out, shaking his head.

"Gonna too cold, no good." He changed the subject. "In school, how much Inupiaq they gonna teaching every day?" He was referring to the Eskimo language. Usually the complaint was that one credit in four years of high school was not enough.

"Maybe one hour a day, Nelson. Not even that much."

"Good, good. Eskimo ways gone now. Gonna need business, teach 'em business. Alaska gonna state now. Pretty soon all under state law. No more gonna hunting, fishing, living like before. Need to learn new way." Nelson's English was so thick and broken that only long acquaintance allowed me to understand. I argued.

"But Nelson, white men brought some bad ways too. Some Eskimo ways are better. Kids should learn both." He laughed, shaking his head.

"Eskimo ways gone. Business. Gonna come roads, gonna come mines. You know it yourself. I know too. Up in Barrow, those people try to go back some ways, but no good." He was referring to the struggle between Native whalers and various outside organizations over Eskimo rights to hunt the endangered bowhead whale. "Whaling almost gone. They tell 'em. Fight all right, but when Alaska gonna state, they can't go back. You know, you see it yourself. I see too."

This from a man who grew up hunting with bow and arrow and nearly starved to death in the mountains thirty years ago. I argued, but he just laughed, that big handsome face squinting in disbelief. Outside his door was a yellow bulldozer and rows of struggling potato plants. Next to the Cat, though, was a drying rack of spruce and willow poles, just as his grandfather might have made. Under a tarp hung split drying fish, a fresh black bear skin, caribou hides, a moose haunch. Down in the eddy the floats of his gillnet twitched with entangled whitefish. Nelson leaned forward, conspiratorial.

"You know this mountain, Ingichuk?" He gestured upward, behind us, where the slope rose out of his field. "Gonna plan. You know how white men ski down mountains? I see on TV." I nodded. "Gonna maybe make ski place here. Cut trees, make ride. Gonna hotel maybe. Good business."

"But Nelson, it's too far. People can ski near Anchorage and lots of other places. This mountain is too small, too." Nelson squinted, laughing gently, shaking his big head at me.

"Gonna come roads. Kotzebue, Ambler, Shungnak gonna bigger, more people. Lots of white people coming. You know for yourself. I know too."

Nelson nodded with satisfaction and sipped his coffee. As always, he knew a good thing when he saw it.

All the Noatagmiut I knew have died, all except me. My grandmother always tell me I should help old people so my life will be longer. Don't make fun of them; if you make fun of them your life will be shorter. I always tried to help old people, bring water to them and meat, so that's why my life is long. My grandmother says that people who try to boss people and not help them, their life will be shorter. My grandmother always tell me if a person come from other place, let him come to your house, give him coffee, tea, or hot water; your life will be longer.

—from the autobiography of
Edna Hunnicutt, *The Eskimo Storyteller,*
by Edwin S. Hall, Jr.

Fire at Us!

▲▲▲▲▲▲▲▲▲▲

I t's a quiet December evening in Ambler, five below zero. As I work at my woodpile, splitting and stacking, I can hear barking sled dogs and the distant clatter of a chain saw. Far overhead, the northern lights flicker across the stars in pale green wraiths.

A snowmobile roars by, going too fast. Kids, I think, and shake my head. Then two more machines follow, and I hear shouts. I drop my ax, trot around the corner of the cabin, and almost slam into Ronald Cleveland, one of my junior high students. Clutching his hat, he's running for his life, and more kids are behind him. "What's going on?" I ask.

"Fire at us!" he yells. "Fire!" I look toward his family's log cabin, 200 yards away through the trees, and see the smoke rising, a glowing white plume against the sky. The breeze shifts, and I'm wrapped in the fire's acrid pall. A neighbor runs by with buckets; I race into my shed to grab mine. As I run down the trail, the village siren wails, sounding the alarm, and all the dogs in town join in, hundreds howling in chorus.

Two dozen people are already at the cabin. More arrive every minute. Most houses in town have a CB radio, and a shouted announcement, "Fire at 73!" has brought everyone running. Some have brought buckets, axes, and fire extinguishers. "Is everyone out?" people ask. "What about the kids?" There were small children inside with a babysitter, and no one knows where they are. Two men try to dash in to check, but gouts of smoke drive them back. There is a moment of panic, and then word is passed along that the children are safe. "*Aarigaa*—that's good!" people nod, relieved.

Dense smoke billows from the door and eaves, but there are no flames showing yet. Clarence steps in with an ax, breaking out a window, and those who have brought their home fire extinguishers step in. When they're done, the smoke seems thicker than ever. A snowmobile pulls up, a trash can full of water in the sled, and the call goes out for more.

"Where's the hydrant?" a man shouts.

"There's nothing," someone answers. As in most bush villages, only a few houses have a fire hydrant nearby, and this cabin is 300 yards off the loop. There is no fire department in Ambler, no truck; only a few coils of hose and a large chemical extinguisher. In an emergency, people must depend on their neighbors and themselves.

Clutching three empty buckets, I ask which nearby house has running water.

"Katherine's," a high school boy says, and we sprint the hundred yards. Rena Cleveland, age ten, answers the door. She points.

"The bathroom's over there!"

"Fill all the pots and pans you can find!" I tell her, and she nods.

Two half-naked toddlers squall on the couch. Rena tells me they were inside the cabin. One of them, playing with matches under a bed, started the fire. My buckets finally full, I race out, sloshing water on the floor. "Never mind!" says Katherine. "Go!"

Outside, the night is bathed in an orange glow; the fire, drafting through the open window, has erupted through the roof and is growing by the second. Following the lead of others, I run to the window, stooping low to escape the heat and smoke, and throw my puny ten gallons into the heart of the flames. There is not even a sizzle. Choking, I stagger away, and another man steps up. The fire ignores us, gathering into a bright roaring pillar as we watch.

"Stand back!" someone shouts, and a snowmobile pulls in, drawing the big chemical extinguisher. Several men wheel it in close and aim the hose. For thirty seconds there is a huge whoosh and a white cloud, and the flames are smothered. The crowd cheers. Then the extinguisher fizzles and sputters out; it was less than half full. We throw all the water we have, then shovelfuls of snow, struggling to hold our advantage, but an orange tongue licks out of the smoke, then another, and the whole roof explodes into fire, driving us back.

I race back for another load of water, stripping off my jacket and fur hat as I run. Katherine and Rena have containers ready, and filling up takes only seconds. Five trips. Six. Each time the flames are higher, the heat more intense. I sling my water and turn to run once more, but Stanley Johnson grabs my arm and shakes his head. "No use, partner. Let it burn." Twenty yards from the blaze, I kneel, coughing and gasping. My coveralls are frozen stiff from spilled water, my face and bare arms scorched. The roof collapses, throwing sparks toward the stars. Far beyond, the aurora pulses its own cold green fire.

Fred and Arlene Greist stand among their friends and relatives, watching all they have disappear. They were hardly wealthy to start with—no savings or insurance—but they had a home, a place they built together, where they raised their children and passed the years. Now, in a matter of minutes, they're down to the clothes they're wearing. Tragedies like this occur everywhere, but here, ringed by wilderness, far beyond the nearest road, the loss seems magnified. The margins of life are thinner, more apparent. As the cabin burns down, it's below zero and falling; without help, the Greist family wouldn't survive the night.

Though there is nothing left to be done, few people leave. All of the *Ivisaappaatmiut* share in the misfortune, offering comfort simply by standing together in the night, bearing witness. Adults talk quietly; children throw chunks of snow into the flames, imitating the fire fighters, pretending that the battle is being won. A beam sags and falls in an explosion of sparks, and the flames flare up again.

The crowd disperses slowly, as if unwilling to admit defeat. Chilled and exhausted, lungs scorched and aching, I head home. A call for assistance goes out on the CB radio. By the time I've changed clothes, Fred and Arlene have been taken in for the night, and offered a vacant house that's actually better than the one they lost. Volunteers go door to door, collecting donations of food, clothing, and cash. People are expected to give what they can. Tomorrow a message will go out on Kotzebue's single radio station, KOTZ, asking for help from the ten villages across the region, and many will respond. I write out a check, stoke my woodstove, and climb into bed, saddened and shaken, yet somehow less alone than before. The fire was "at us." We were all there.

Animals have souls. If people don't cut it in the throat the animal won't go away. Anything they catch they have to cut the throat. It's wrong to work on animal skins with meat still on them because they have a soul.

—from the autobiography of
Edna Hunnicutt, *The Eskimo Storyteller,*
by Edwin S. Hall, Jr.

Traveling Like Clarence

▲▲▲▲▲▲▲▲

I'm losing speed. I rock side to side and lean forward over my snowmobile's skis, but it's no use. I'm going down. The engine screams, straining against the sled. Then the track spins free and I sink in a spray of waist-deep snow. *Here we go again.* I find my pliers and twist the hitch pin. The machine roars out with a grunt and a shove, but the sled is another story. Lugged down by forty gallons of gas and a week's worth of camping gear—canvas wall tent, airtight woodstove, food, sleeping bags, clothing, rifle, spare parts, tools—the eight-foot freighter is nearly buried. I plant my heels and heave, but it won't budge. The whole thing weighs close to seven hundred pounds; short of unloading, there's nothing to do but dig out the runners and wait. It's warm for late March—a bit below zero—and I'm sweating in my heavy coveralls. A cow moose and calf gawk from the willows, then trot off down the Ambler River, hackles raised in indignation.

At last I hear the whine of an engine, and Clarence loops around the bend, traveling fast. It's the third time in five miles that he's had to drop his own sled and double back to help.

"Clarence, I'm sorry."

"It's all right," he says with a shrug. His weather-scarred Eskimo face is relaxed, without a hint of impatience, even though he's been breaking trail with a load heavier than mine. But there is something in his eyes more terrible than anger. I can feel him sizing me up with ruthless clarity, the way a wolf looks over a moose.

"Your sled's too short, I guess." His own fourteen-foot basket sled, an intricate construction of hardwood lathe and nylon twine, floats effortlessly where mine sinks.

I protest eloquently in my sled's defense. It's my child; I designed and built it myself. Clarence just shrugs. As we're struggling, I hear him mutter to himself, "Too short."

We're only twenty miles into the trip. Clarence is headed for the village of Anaktuvuk Pass, 250 miles to the northeast, and I'm going halfway to the upper Noatak, where I plan to spend a week before doubling back to Ambler. I have enough gas to cover 500 miles. There are no villages on the way, and we're unlikely to meet anyone on the trail. The Kobuk Inupiat venture into the heart of the western Brooks Range only to hunt, and seldom stay long. I carry a few maps but no compass, figuring I know the country well enough to navigate by the proper USGS quadrant. Clarence's map is in his head.

The logistics are beyond those of normal trips—hunting caribou, hauling firewood, or driving to Shungnak. We're headed past the range of the village search-and-rescue teams, where most *Ivisaappaatmiut* don't consider venturing. No practical reason drives anyone to travel this far, and the subsistence lifestyle, by definition, roots itself in necessity. Clarence can say he's delivering a hardwood sled he's made to a buyer in Anaktuvuk Pass, but the cost of gas, oil, food, and snowmobile parts—several hundred dollars each way—eats most of his profit. These long trips, which he takes once or twice a year, are more like pilgrimages. "Real good country up there," he says, and that's enough reason for both of us to go.

We swing off the heavily timbered Ambler River, northward up the tundra of the Redstone valley toward Ivishak Pass, following a route Clarence first showed me eleven years ago. "Old timers' sled dog trail," he tells me, pointing to a scarred spruce trunk. Old timers: the generations of Inupiat who came before, people who moved and breathed with the land and left few signs of their passing—chips of stone and bone, scattered house pits and fire rings. "Tough sonofabitches, I tell you," Clarence murmurs.

In the last sheltered clump of trees, just below Ivishak, we stop to top off our gas tanks, check the sleds, and pull up our parka hoods. Clear weather here means a savage headwind blasting down the pass. Once we start climbing, there will be no place to stop or rest for eight miles. Ahead we can see a plume of windblown snow billowing into the valley, high enough to obscure the mountain beyond.

Slamming over rock-hard drifts, we fight uphill and upstream against a howling river of white. The pass rises steadily, narrowing like a throat, pinnacles of rock looming on either side. I crouch behind the windshield, strain my breath through clenched teeth, and run by feel more than sight in the worst gusts—forty, fifty miles an hour. My cheeks go dead as the sled fishtails and pounds. Far above, through a veil of windblown snow, the sky is blue and serene. The sun is shining. Two miles. Five. I glimpse the crest of the pass, a last pitch of deep snow. I lean forward, yank the throttle, and hold on. The machine bucks and screams, less than a quarter-mile to go. Just as I congratulate myself, the sled gives a sickening lurch and bogs down. I leap off, tugging and cursing, but it's no use. One runner has dug in, and blowing snow is already making a drift out of my machine. I'm tempted to shoot myself rather than face Clarence again, with those cold wolf eyes that measure without anger. Then I make out a dark shape a hundred yards ahead. It's Clarence, and he's stuck, too. I breathe a sigh of relief, and scramble to help *him*.

After thirty minutes of ferrying small loads over the top, we stand on the crest of Ivishak, repacking our sleds. The wind here is only twenty miles an hour or so, and it will fade as we draw away from the pass. Ahead stretches the Cutler valley. From now on, we're beyond the trees, and their absence is startling. The universe is suddenly unbroken, white, endless. Mountains sweep up on either side and fade off to the horizon, framing a corridor leading north. "Should be good trail," says Clarence. "Ready?"

For the next twenty miles we make time over windpacked drifts; as I jounce along, I try to visualize our way through the maze ahead, which I've traveled several times over the years: right off the Cutler against the sharp dark cliff I call the Pyramid; then a stretch of high, rolling tundra, climbing steadily through deep, drifted snow where willows rise like black fingers, down again and across the blue overflow ice of Amakomanaq Creek, up a long grade and down into a canyon for a few miles; then over a mountain and across the Imelyak valley; another narrow canyon, and a twisting drop to the wide tundra flats of the Noatak.

I suddenly realize that, while I'm following his trail, Clarence has pulled away and is nowhere in sight. I shake my head, lean into the throttle for a few miles, and finally spot him. He's smoking a cigarette and knocking ice off his undercarriage, killing time, waiting for me.

"What happened?" he asks. "Get stuck?"

"Just a little," I say, and change the subject.

We make camp in a brushy creek bottom. In this country, you can't stop just anywhere; mountain squalls can erupt without warning and flatten a tent, and there are places, like Ivishak, where prevailing winds are funneled to gale force. The other requisite is wood—enough dry willow sticks to feed the stove. Clarence knows dozens of spots, some passed down for generations and others he discovered himself.

Snug in our canvas tent, I study my USGS map quadrants, based on federal surveys and aerial photographs, with contours and vegetation marked in brown and green. While Clarence is interested, I can also tell he's amused that I need them. I have thousands of square miles spread before me, and if I point to a creek—any creek—on any map, Clarence will first offer whether it's useful for travel, and then he'll point out camping places. Then he'll say, "I get brown bear there one time," or, "That one can never freeze good. Danger." His topographical vision is intimate, exact, as if he'd been a raven in a past life and looked down on it all.

We share food and coffee, and I try to keep Clarence talking. How many wolves has he shot in his life? What year did he get his first snowmobile? What does he think about the village schools, and the way things have changed? I want to know what he knows, and, even more, what he thinks. Clarence answers patiently for a while, then gradually falls silent. Too many questions, I know, is considered rude, and I've been pushing my luck.

As I unpack my sleeping gear—double down bags, acrylic fleece suit, and two sleeping pads—I can feel him watching me. I look up and he shakes his head. "Too much."

"What?"

"Too much sleeping bag." The one he's unrolled has ducks and dogs on a red flannel liner, like kids use for backyard slumber parties.

"Too much clothes. Look at me. That's all you need." He's stripped to a pair of cotton gym socks, white cotton T-shirt, and briefs. He crawls into his bag without long johns or even a hat on his shaved head (hair that needs combing and washing is just another encumbrance), and rolls up his corduroy slacks and flannel shirt for a pillow. The outside temperature is below zero and falling. He grins at me, half teasing, half serious. "Too much. Just leave it by the trail in the morning. You should travel like me."

"Clarence, I'd freeze to death."

He squints, laughs, and rolls over. "Good night, partner."

He's awake by seven. "Where's the coffee?" he asks.

I know that camp chores are my duty; traditionally, a young man serves as apprentice to a more experienced hunter, and shows respect by serving him. I shiver as the stove crackles to life, then duck outside for more wood. Though our little valley lies in cold shadow, the mountains glow in the rising sun. Ptarmigan chuckle in the willows twenty yards away, and whir into flight.

Clarence is quiet this morning. Then again, he's usually that way. Even if he stops by my cabin in town to pay a social call, he'll sometimes sit without speaking, with no sign of discomfort no matter how long the silence continues. It seems to be a stillness born of the land, of a life spent listening, watching, and waiting. I've often tried to imitate this quiet, but that's all it is—an imitation. We sit eating oatmeal and drinking coffee, listening to the stove hiss. Finally he lifts his cup, nods to himself and says, "Too much think about bullshit. That's what makes you nervous."

For a moment I'm nonplussed, not sure what he's talking about. Then I remember: my questions last night regarding Inupiat culture, philosophy, and the future. Asking about a canyon or a river was one thing; asking if he worried about the changing world was another. Clarence's vast knowledge is anchored in the practical and the immediate—reading snow conditions, building sleds, picking out the best caribou from a herd. Abstract notions are superfluous; no, worse. Bullshit. The Inupiaq language, I remind myself, has no future tense.

We break camp quickly, working barehanded on the tent ropes, and again as we tie down our gear. After five minutes at ten below zero, my fingers go dead; I have to unzip my parka and shove them into my armpits. As half-frozen nerves waken, the pain is electric. Clarence looks up and sees me wincing. "Your hands are cold?" he asks. The incredulity in his voice suggests he'd just heard that Martians had landed up the creek. At first I think he's poking fun at me, but the surprise seems genuine. He purses his lips and seems thoughtful as he helps me cinch down my load.

For the next fifteen miles the snow is hard and smooth, the driving almost effortless as we cross the high tundra sweep of Amakomanaq. Fog clings to the land, casting a luminous, transparent glow that seems to come from inside everything. Ordinary objects—willows, rocks, my gloved hands—are suffused with a subtle brilliance, so purely etched that their beauty becomes almost painful. Ahead, the jagged peaks of the Imelyak float like clouds, their distance and size impossible to determine. We roar along, wrapped in a silver blanket of light.

On the north side of the Imelyak valley we enter a narrow canyon, the only one that goes through to the Noatak. The passage is far from obvious; the canyon mouth, maybe fifty yards wide, strewn with boulders, seems to promise a dead end. The snow is sparse and windblown as we thread between willows and rocks, rattle over gravel. The mountains enclose us, but always there is a pathway leading north. I imagine a lone hunter, clad in caribou skins and clutching a spear, discovering this route for the first time, reveling in its unfolding. And now we follow his trail, passed down for centuries from fathers to sons. Though Clarence has told me he plans to show his boys the way, he hasn't done it yet; he seems unwilling or unable to drag them away from the gym and television for more than a day or two, and then there's the expense of two machines on a long trip. But I can't help wishing that Floyd and Luke were here instead of me, and wondering if they ever will be.

Clarence stops. As I pull up, I see what he sees—fresh wolf tracks, broad as my palm. "Two of them," he says. "This morning. Going Noatak, same as us." He shrugs casually and snaps a loaded clip into his carbine.

These aren't the first tracks we've crossed, and I can't tell the difference between these and others he's barely glanced at. The chance of spotting their makers is slim; I've gone entire winters without seeing one wolf, even when their tracks were everywhere. But now there is an expectant lean to Clarence's shoulders as he rides, scanning the trail ahead.

The canyon rises into a narrow pass, and beyond lies the Noatak. Clarence slows and motions me over. "Unhitch your sled. Up there." I follow his point, and, on the crest of a ridge a quarter mile off, a black wolf stands silhouetted against the sky. It regards us for a moment, then trots over the top. "You go around that way, I'll go this side. Should be pretty nice." He checks his rifle, guns the throttle, and vaults uphill in a cloud of snow.

On the far side of the ridge I find a maze of wolf and snowmobile tracks, but no Clarence. Angling east for a mile, I finally spot him and catch up. He shakes his head, disgusted. "Lost them somewhere," he mutters. Just then a distant flicker of motion catches his eye. "What's that, fox? No, wolf!" And he's gone again. Driving like a fool, I almost manage to keep up as he slams downhill and flies across a stretch of overflow ice, the wolf bounding ahead at thirty miles an hour, running tail out, then floundering in a patch of soft snow. Clarence slews to a stop, raises his carbine, and fires. The wolf, a large gray female, drops in its tracks, paws splayed, as if clubbed. I know I'd have missed the same shot ten times over. "Pretty good," says Clarence, lighting a cigarette. "Let's go back to the sleds and skin *this*." He seems to avoid the word "wolf" deliberately, though I don't ask. A century ago, an Inupiat hunter wouldn't think of uttering the name of the animal he sought or had just killed, lest it should hear and think him boastful.

As I make coffee in a sheltered patch of willows, Clarence neatly rolls up his sleeves and sharpens his knife. "Keep your eye out for the black one," He says. "He'll come back for his woman." I hope to myself that the black one has the common sense to disappear over the next mountain. Although the smoke-gray pelt Clarence pares away is rich and luxurious by itself, it contains only a whisper of the grace and spirit that was held within. And yet, if anyone on the planet has a right to a wolf, it's Clarence, who has lived and hunted with them all his life. He certainly has no regret about killing her, or any animal he or his family needs. When he looks down at the stiff, flayed carcass, the blood on the snow, he sees only good fortune. As a fellow predator, the wolf would understand. This is my problem, culturally and philosophically. I know what Clarence would say. *Too much think about bullshit.*

I look up to tell Clarence the coffee's ready, and there, on a tundra hill, is the black wolf. Though it's more than a half mile away, there's no mistaking the loosefooted trot, the thick, brushy tail. I consider saying nothing, but I know that Clarence will spot it any minute. It crosses my mind, too, to tell him and let him go first. But I already know what I want—to show him that I can do something right, that I'm a worthy partner, a success in terms he'll understand. It's not just this trip; around Clarence I've always felt that I'm a day late and a dollar short. The things I've succeeded at—teaching, coaching basketball, writing—mean nothing to him. I unhitch my sled and see to my rifle. Then I say, "Wolf. There."

I drive carefully, using the terrain to keep out of sight, trying to imagine where the wolf will be. I move up a gully, cross a low ridge into the next creek, and ease over the rise. The wolf, aware but not startled, stands a hundred yards away. Shakily I raise my rifle, find his shoulder in the crosshairs, and fire. He gives a leap of surprise, staggers, and gathers himself. Then he's running, flowing uphill, headed for the next ridge and the mountain beyond. Sickness and elation rise in my throat. I see blood flecks in his trail.

Two miles later, on the far side of the mountain, I find him. As I approach, the wolf rises from the willows and fixes me in a yellow stare. Fifty feet away, he seems beautifully surreal, a luminous shadow poised on the edge of flight. His shoulder is wet with blood, and the steam of his breath pulses into the cold. I want to talk to him, to explain that if I could, I would take my bullet back. Head low, hackles raised, he measures me, unafraid and unforgiving. I hear the whine of an engine. Clarence is coming. I aim behind the ear and fire.

Clarence pulls up. "I went wrong way round the mountain," he says. "Good for you." Those three words and a nod are, for him, lavish praise. I've done well.

As we pound across the rock-hard drifts of the Noatak flats, I'm pursued by the skinned wolf carcasses lying side by side in the little creek bottom, legs outstretched, lidless eyes staring, teeth bared in lipless snarls. Useless as food, we've left them behind. Though Clarence made sure the throats were cut—*nigiluq*, ensuring that their souls could escape and be reborn, more wolves to hunt—I'm not comforted. *Good for you*, Clarence had said. Knowing what I do now, I'm even less sure. For, returning alone over that same trail a week later, I would find wolf trails converging on that spot, and a ring of depressions around the carcasses, marking where six wolves had sat with their dead. I can't say that they came to mourn, but I know that they approached from different directions singly and in pairs; that some came close to sniff the bodies; that all sat within a ten foot circle and left together, a single column heading west. None of the tracks were as large as the black wolf's had been.

We make camp in a small canyon below Douglas Creek. A wall of black rock rises behind us; a pair of gyrfalcons keen as they circle overhead. Clarence calls the place Spring, and points to the Dall sheep that are drawn here by the water that seeps from the rocks, even in winter. The rams peer down at us, then return to their grazing. As we shovel out a spot for the tent, I feel lightheaded and vaguely ill. Then I'm on my knees, clutching my shovel.

"You all right?" Clarence asks.

"Just tired," I say.

In the morning Clarence packs his sled. It's still one hundred twenty-five miles to Anaktuvuk Pass, and he hopes to make it today. I decide to go along as far as the Nigu River, in part because I want to learn the trail, and also because Clarence's drive clutch is acting up. This is our point of maximum isolation, more than a hundred miles to the nearest help, and the next thirty miles are mostly uphill. If he's going to break down, it will probably be on this stretch. As we travel up Douglas Creek, Clarence stops several times to tinker under the cowling, but finally shakes his head. "Just worn out, I guess." His Arctic Cat, not a year old, has nearly eight thousand miles on its odometer—eight thousand miles of heavy sleds and forty below, far beyond the manufacturer's expectations. He talks about rebuilding it, but next year he'll have a new machine.

We cut through a narrow pass into the headwaters of Midas Creek, named a century ago by white prospectors. As we bear northeast, the country becomes increasingly windblown and barren, a labyrinth of seemingly identical hills and creeks. Though I concentrate, I can't keep them straight. I'm not even sure a map and compass would help here. I stay right behind Clarence, glad I'll have our trail to follow back. "Good hunting country," Clarence says. "Wide open."

The traveling is smooth, and an hour later we're facing the ragged blue spires of the Nigu valley. Here, on the crest of a windswept pass, Clarence and I will part. He checks his clutch once more, and we eat—frozen cheese, dry caribou meat, and coffee. A few years ago, Clarence says, he blew his engine here and was eventually rescued by Anaktuvuk trappers.

"What if they hadn't come by?" I ask.

Clarence shrugs. "I don't know."

"Well," says Clarence, "Time to go." He still has a hundred miles ahead, driving into the wind. He lights a cigarette and looks north toward the Nigu. "Good trail," he says. "Good weather. I don't give a shit about nothing." With wraparound Ray-Bans and a Marlboro cocked in one corner of his dark, weatherbeaten face, his offhand bravado seems both gallant and vaguely comical. I sit astride my idling machine, watching him prepare, feeling the distance. He tops off his gas tank, tightens his sled ropes. Then Clarence gives a broad smile, pulls off his glove, and extends his hand. "Take it easy, my friend."

I pull off my own glove and nod, quietly overcome by that simple declaration, offered in the wind and silence.

Cigarette dangling, Clarence guns his engine and roars off down the slope. As I watch, he dwindles to a dark speck, slides over a rise, and vanishes into the folds of the land.

I had to drag my own father through the water to the graveyard in Kotzebue. The people wouldn't help me. Dogs ate him. When Robert Sams [sic] (the first missionary) came he told me not to cry for my father because he was already in heaven. That's why I tried to be Christian too.

. . . About two months after that a man died and they buried him in a box. Now they always do that."

—from the autobiography of
Edna Hunnicutt, *The Eskimo Storyteller*,
by Edwin S. Hall, Jr.

Sharing the Weight

▲▲▲▲▲▲▲▲

In January's deep cold and darkness is more darkness. Dan Denslow is dead, and five others with him: six dead from the neighboring villages of Ambler and Shungnak, from a population of five hundred. Almost every family has lost a husband, a wife, an uncle, a cousin, a friend, a childhood playmate. The grief hangs like ice fog in the still January air.

It was a plane crash. These accidents are occasional facts of life in a land without roads, where everybody depends on small planes; this crash, though, is the worst in the history of the northwest arctic. And Dan, with fourteen years of flying experience in the Kobuk valley, was perhaps the best pilot in the region—careful, deliberate, meticulous. But an error in judgment combined with bad luck, and his Cessna 185 crashed and burned at the Shungnak airstrip.

Dan didn't want to fly that day. It was too cold, he said; forty below at noon, not unusual for the upper Kobuk in early January. Most pilots put the limit around minus thirty, the point where gasoline stops vaporizing. Even cold gas will burn inside a hot engine, but fuel filters and lines can get clogged with ice crystals, and the chance of stalling is much greater. Gas isn't the only problem in deep cold. Everything gets brittle—plastics, even steel. Dan knew all this. He had no reason to push it. Actually, he was out of the air taxi business; he'd sold his Ambler Air license to Dave Rue. But just now Dave was headed to Fairbanks on business, and Dan was filling in. Since he was the only licensed air-taxi pilot in the upper Kobuk, Charlie Douglas and the others came to him.

They wanted to go to Shungnak for a funeral. An old man had died, and they, as kinsmen, felt the obligation to go—obligation, not desire. Even distant cousins who had never met the deceased, even those who were not related by blood but bearing the same first name as the dead one—*atins,* namesakes—should go. Since Shungnak was just twenty-two miles upriver, the pull was especially strong. Myrna Cleveland, with her infant and two young children, obviously couldn't make the overland ride in this cold, and the others had their reasons—not enough warm clothing or lack of a good machine; some just wanted to fly because they had the money. They kept asking Dan. It was only a fifteen-minute flight. The funeral would start in a few hours.

Dan understood their obligation, but he also understood the cold. He said he'd fly if it warmed up a little. But Dan had known Charlie Douglas for years, and Charlie kept asking, and Dan finally agreed, though the thermometer hadn't budged upward, and might not for days. Just this once. After all, it was just a fifteen-minute hop. He told his wife, Joyce, that he'd be back as soon as he could.

Getting ready in this kind of cold takes time. Dan set up his engine heater and let it run for a half hour, defrosted his windows, checked the fuel, and made double sure that the filters were clear. The 185 is a good, dependable plane, and Dan maintained his carefully. That's one secret of safe flying.

Eight people showed up. The plane, equipped with a bench seat in the back, was rated to carry five. Dan didn't like flying overloaded. If he got caught, they could pull his license, and there was the matter of insurance. Charlie and the others pleaded. Three of the passengers were children who could sit on laps, and it was just a short flight. Dan relented. The light was already fading, and it was too cold to stand around talking. They needed to get going.

Fitting everyone and their bags in the Cessna took some doing. The big Continental engine could lift about anything; space was the limiting factor. Somehow everybody got crammed in, people and knapsacks shoved into every free space. As the 185 lifted off, the propeller cutting the air with its wide wail, the windows were already fogging up. In five minutes, the only view was through a narrow swatch of windshield, a foot square, cleared by the pilot's defroster. In the gray, fading light and the ice fog below, there wasn't much to see, anyway. It would be another day before the sun would clear the horizon.

At Shungnak, people were listening for the plane. Snow machines and sleds idled outside, wrapped in thick plumes of exhaust. Smoke from chimneys clung to the rooftops, unable to rise, too heavy with ice crystals. The temperature was not forty but fifty below now, and falling. People heard the engine's drone and got their parkas and boots on. They wanted to be there to meet the plane; it was a part of funeral decorum.

Those who were not riding a machine heard the Cessna's engine stutter, catch, and die, and the whistle of air over the wings as the plane glided down, losing altitude quickly. If Dan had been able to see on all sides, he might have made a dead stick landing on the strip, or guided the plane onto an open stretch of tundra. Fighting the controls and the panic of the passengers, peering through his tiny cleared patch of glass into an onrushing gray-white blur, he probably never saw the berm— the five-foot wall of snow cleared from the runway. Angling into the strip at a hundred miles an hour, his landing gear caught. The plane pitched nose down as the gear sheared away, dragging down a wing. Torn back as the plane slammed along, the wing and the full fuel tank inside it ruptured—and then there was a ball of flame.

At least some of the passengers survived the impact, but they were battered, and the front doors were jammed. People raced to the wreck, but the flames rolled out, driving them back. They could only stand there and watch the plane burn, listening to the high-pitched screams inside. Myrna Cleveland staggered out of the flames with her baby, parka and hair burning, and collapsed under the wing. Then there was an explosion, and the screams stopped. The fireball drove the rescuers back, faces singed, parkas smoking. They stood helpless as Dan's Cessna burned to a husk. By the time fire extinguishers arrived, it was too late.

As the flames died, someone heard whimpering from the drifted snow near the berm. One of Myrna's children lay nearly buried, a leg broken. They bundled her up and rushed her to the village as searchers combed the plane's crash path. They found Myrna's boy, beaten up and half frozen but still breathing. The two children had been sitting on laps in the back seat, outside the single belt that held the others down. The impact had sprung the rear door, and they had been thrown clear. They were the only survivors.

The Federal Aviation Administration investigators have come and gone; they took pictures, sifted through the wreck for telling fragments, and left. Their eventual ruling: pilot error. The engine probably stopped due to ice buildup in the fuel filters, but the official blame rests with Dan. If you read the official accident reports from all the Alaskan air crashes over the years, the phrase repeats: Pilot error. Pilot error.

The bodies were flown to Anchorage for autopsy, then returned. The plywood coffins the village men built would be strangely shaped: two almost square, over three feet wide and not five feet long. They would have to be that shape to fit what was left of Charlie Douglas and Dan Denslow. Somehow the two bodies were mislabeled. The mistake was set right only when someone recognized Dan's ring. Myrna and her baby, fused in death, would share the same coffin.

The funeral for the Shungnak dead was two days before Ambler's service. I flew in on the Munz Airlines mail plane from Kotzebue. The fifteen-seat cabin was full but quiet during the two-hour flight except for the occasional whimper of a child. Then, as we descended near Shungnak, it started. A young woman began in low, long moans, and a woman in the back joined in a cry of *adiiii*. The teenage boy next to me began a noise deep in his throat, and then it was everyone, children wailing, an old man staring out of the window, his *aahhhh* just audible above the engines. Until the jolt of landing we were joined, though each sang alone.

For a week people have been gathering in Ambler—several planeloads a day, and caravans of snow machines up the river. People have come from Minnesota, Arizona, Oklahoma, from all across Alaska, and from the ten northwest arctic villages. Normally, 250-odd people live in Ambler, but the population has more than doubled. Every house is full. They are here to reestablish bonds of kinship and to pay last respects; but what they have truly come for is to share the weight of grief. Strangers console each other; enemies shake hands.

Some of the village men work through the night making the coffins and crosses, and others dig the graves, a long, cold process when the ground is hard from months of subzero weather. They build a fire to thaw a layer of soil, move the coals and scoop the loose dirt out, then move the fire back—over and over. It takes a full day to dig four feet, with most able-bodied men and boys taking a turn. The women cook—huge kettles of caribou soup, countless loaves of bread, gallons of coffee. They sit together in groups and mourn. Some weep quietly, and others twine their voices in anguish. The death songs carry through walls, float through the ice fog to those passing by in the stiff afternoon darkness.

Funerals here, like everywhere, mean drinking. Those who do so drink hard, day and night; they may or may not sober up for the actual funeral. Ambler is dry, but the planes and snow machines from Kotzebue guarantee plenty of booze in town. Bacardi 151 is the drink of choice. Around here, you drink like you mean it or you don't drink at all; drink until it's gone, and then look for more. This time, though, the drinking circle is smaller than usual, and the binges shorter; even the hard-core funeral drunks are too overcome to attempt escape.

The Friends Church and the community building become the center of everything. Pastors from villages across the region come, and there are prayer meetings and services every day at the log church on the river bank. There is always hot coffee at "the community," and most travelers stop there first. The local brand of evangelical Quakerism, always a force, now rules the village. There are tearful testimonials and conversions, especially among the young, and Bibles are carried everywhere. In a month or two, many of the new converts will slip away, gradually losing interest, but just now they seek the light in droves. Death leans in, and no one wants to face it unprepared.

Before the *naluaqmiut* brought their ways and their God to the Kobuk valley a hundred years ago, life was harder and death was darker; the elders will tell you. The people were scattered across the valleys in small nomadic bands of one or two families. Sickness or hunger could decimate a camp, even wipe it out, and the deaths might go undiscovered for months. When a band was on the move, pushing upriver before the ice came or trying to find caribou, survival of the group came first. If an old woman was too weak to keep up, she expected the others to leave her. A daughter might stay behind, but if she did, it was her sacrifice and risk, a display of devotion. The others would push on. The spirits of the dead were powerful, and not even a shaman, an *anjatkut,* could safely tend to a dying person. If someone witnessed a death, he or she was contaminated, and had to stay away from the others for four days. It was the law of the shamans. No one wanted to be alone with the weight of death, so even if a group were not on the move, a person was often left to die alone.

Afterward there was no such thing as a funeral service or a dug grave. The body was placed on a worn-out animal skin or on a sled and dragged away for the foxes and ravens; occasionally a teepee of spruce poles might be built, and the body placed inside with a few prized possessions. Fearing the power of the dead, no one lingered. Perhaps the excess of modern Eskimo funerals is a reaction to this past, when death was so lonely.

The service is in the school gymnasium; it is the only building large enough. With all the bleachers filled, and chairs jammed in rows on the basketball court, there is barely space for everyone. People are seated by blood or group: the white community in a tier on the left, close kin of the dead front and center, the local National Guard on the right (Charlie Douglas was a staff sergeant), a hiearchy of blood relatives behind the immediate family, then general seating. Three caskets rest on sawhorses, nailed shut, topped with framed photos and plastic flowers. There are two wreaths of genuine blossoms, flown up from hothouses a thousand miles to the south. Behind a podium are six Friends Church pastors, and an old man hunched over an electric organ stumbles through a featureless melody. No one is wearing a suit. There are a few ties and a dress or two, but most wear everyday clothing—jeans, flannel shirts, parkas, mukluks, calico pullovers.

There is some weeping, but most sit quietly. When a toddler escapes his mother and runs out to the podium, everyone laughs. Last night there was a wake at the church with testimonials, and most are cried out. Most of this service is music; the school staff, city league basketball teams, the National Guard, the Kiana and Shungnak people, the church youth group—everyone gets up front and sings once, or several times. The singing is off-key for the most part, and the hymns all sound the same: lyrics about the rewards of heaven and the endless travail below. But the important thing is that everyone has a part; everyone shares the load.

Preachers deliver impassioned messages of mortality and salvation. One shouts repeatedly, "I love Jesus, and I can't wait to die!" But then Kaye Rue, wife of Dan's partner, sings "How Great Thou Art" in a crystalline soprano. As she finishes, there is the full silence of five hundred people hanging on her last note. Joyce, Dan's widow, reads his favorite poem, about a pilot reaching out and touching the face of God. Her voice is clear and strong, but then, as she gives a simple apology on behalf of Dan, she breaks. Bessie, Charlie's widow, a short, dark, middle-aged woman with a face past grief, goes to her, embraces her, and she finishes. The two widows stand, arms locked, facing everyone, staring into nothing.

To end the service, everyone files past the coffins, pausing to touch the lids or look at the photos. The organ plays quietly, and a voice rises above it. Maude Foxglove, Charlie's ancient, nearly blind mother, keens a dirge without words, a high, wavering cry that fills the room, rising and falling like distant wind, the cry of those who have walked on in the snow, leaving their children under caribou hides. When I imagine that time, it is her voice I hear.

As the light fades there is a snow machine procession to the graves, a mile out of town. The knoll is crowned with aspen and birch, and faces the white crags of the Jade Mountains. On the other side is the rolling expanse of the Kobuk valley: a stretch of spruce forest, tundra, and the hills beyond—a good place to become part of, a good place to wait. The old belief was that spirits rose into the sky to dance in the aurora, awaiting the birth of children to bear their names, to become vessels for their souls. Even today a family's first child born after a death carries the dead one's name—and, some insist, the same spirit.

There are only six other graves here; Ambler is a new village, settled only twenty-odd years now. In time, the knoll will fill up. A white picket fence surrounds the graves, three of which are raised mounds with galvanized tin roofs, graves dug in winter. They are garlanded with plastic flowers and marked by wooden crosses. A military guard of honor fires a parting salute: two volleys for a staff sergeant. Preachers speak, heads bow, caskets are covered with frozen clods as best as they can be. No one stays long. The wind blows cold off the Jade Mountains, and spring is three months away.

At other times bears take away people when they find them asleep. A person caught in his sleep must pretend that he is dead even though the bear swings him around.

The Ipani Eskimo tell their children, "Do not boast and say that you can lick a bear any time you see him." Bears want to catch boasters unaware, and many a time it ends up a fatal injury to the boaster when the bear finds him.

—James Wells, *Ipani Eskimos*

An Amulet of the Spirit

▲▲▲▲▲▲▲▲▲

T he gravel bar was nothing special—a gibbous curve fringed by scrub willow and littered with gray skeletons of spruce. Heading upstream in my jetboat, no destination in particular, I almost skidded past. But the day was almost over. Ahead, I knew, lay a maze of rocky channels. Here was a good tent site, wood, a pool full of rising grayling, and, just across the river, a slope grooved with caribou trails.

Unloading the boat, I moved deliberately, avoiding clanks on the hull. Without the roar of the outboard jet, there was only the cold music of the river and the hiss of distance. I pitched my tent on a level, sandy patch with a good view of the hill. The long open slope was still lit like a stage, and I swung in a rhythm of working and watching. There, a white shimmer a half mile away. Caribou. A small band of cows trotted south, dropped down into a creekbed, and disappeared.

Gathering firewood, I saw the first tracks. A big grizzly's, but more than a week old—indistinct edges, rainwashed. Ancient history. The sound of the motor, I told myself, would have been enough to roust any bear out of the neighborhood. Down the bar were more trails: moose, wolf, caribou, fox, two different black bears. Many had not been rained on, and some were only hours old. This narrow curve of gravel, through some synergy of topography and time, was a game highway at rush hour. I'd found the right place to see things, and that's what I'd come for.

I walked on, feeling pretty good until I found the first salmon carcass. At the tail of the bar were other salmon—or parts of them. And there, in a patch of wet silt, were grizzly prints so fresh that the whorls and grooves of his toes were captured as if he'd walked through ink.

The rear paw was almost as long, and spread twice the width of my own size eleven. Not the tracks of any bear. This was The Bear, the one that lurked in the closet and prowled my darkened bedroom when I was six. I'd seen big tracks before, but never so fresh, so close to camp with night closing in.

Of course I considered moving—screw the tent, get out of here! But then, walking back toward camp, a round chambered in my rifle, jittering at every dark shape, I knew that I'd come here for one reason: to meet The Bear up close.

The fact that it happened the way it was supposed to was what caught me. I just looked across the river and there he was, head down in a blueberry patch, rump framed by an opening in the brush. My pulse thundered up like a cloud of birds. Destiny took form in that immense mound of fur, so close I could have bounced a rock off it.

My next impulse was simple and direct: Shoot. Now. It—he— was just too close. The few yards of gravel and knee-deep water weren't enough if he decided to charge. I'd been charged before, but always with a partner nearby. Alone was different. I flicked off the safety switch and waited for him to turn broadside. The barrel wavered with each heartbeat.

He turned, haloed in silver as the light caught him. Pale flanks merged into chocolate forelegs, and the markings on his haunches rippled into an almost white shoulder hump and head—a head as wide as my chest, set on a muscled torso Michaelangelo would have understood. Through the scope I could see his eyes. They weren't what I'd expected—not piglike, as bears' eyes so often seem at the instant of confrontation, the face tensed in curiosity, surprise, or anger. These eyes were wide, delicately lashed, beautiful in a quite feminine way, and here, in this abundance of berries and salmon, the sun fading, they radiated a serenity we, for all our anthropomorphic generosity, reserve for human saints. He hadn't sensed me, and I had the crosshairs fixed behind his ear.

He meandered back and forth, head down, jaws working, sprawl- ing face-first in a blue patch, arms spread, and then up, moving concentric ripples radiating from neck to rump as if he were growing with each mouthful. Waddling with fat, only a few weeks from winter denning, he moved with economical grace, each movement connected perfectly to the next. Fear faded into fascination, and I forgot things—

forgot I was watching through the scope of a high-powered rifle, forgot the finger on the trigger and the shell nestled in the chamber, a twitch away from explosion. For a time all I knew of the world was a bear shining in the dusk.

And then, gradually, I became aware of a whisper from inside: It's beautiful. Shoot it. I knew how easy it would be—the heart, there; the spine, there. I had the power to reach across the river with a godlike fist. I saw the dazzling pelt spread across my cabin floor, far more than a rug to admire, an amulet of the spirit inside it—something rare, beyond artifice, caught and held, and so somehow owned.

I hadn't planned on killing a grizzly—in fact had, four years ago, decided I wouldn't kill another—but that was a different valley, a different time, a different bear. Rational thought moved in like a lawyer gathering up loose ends. It was, after all, bear season, and I had a hunting license in my pocket, a rifle in my hands, and the bear of a lifetime filling the scope. The grizzly tag was a twenty-five dollar formality I could take care of later. Why not? There were plenty of bears, and one this large was bound to be old, probably suffering from arthritis and bad teeth. The same destiny that brought us together might mean for me to pull the trigger. Why not?

I braced again, elbows on knees, the stock smooth against my cheek. The bear was still foraging. My hands were ice-calm now as I waited for a clear shot. He swung broadside at last, absorbed in digging out a squirrel hole. I held low on the front shoulder and drew in a breath. Steady.

Then he looked up, ears cocked as he peered across the river. He couldn't have heard me or seen me, hunkered in the willows. The wind was wrong for a scent. Yet he stared straight toward where I sat, tilting his head as if puzzled. Then he lowered his head and went back to digging.

That night I lay awake, listening to the tent flex and rustle in the wind. Somewhere in the darkness, not far off, The Bear was roaming, and I lay with blood rushing in my ears, a child again in a vast dark room, waiting for a bump in the night. Wrapped in the comforting blanket of my fear, I smiled. And after a long time, I slept.

*Undaunted, the two orphans decided to enter the
structure. In, through the stormshed, they entered and
climbed up through the main entrance. It was a large
circular house with platform benches along the walls of
each side. Seated close together on either side were big
men with disfigured faces, their mouths and facial
muscles twisted in every which way. The circular house
had living quarters on either side. Way in the back sat a
man. He was sitting on the floor. He said to them, "Seat
yourselves on the* akisaun *of the platform bench." They
sat down where he had requested. Although the ones
sitting on the benches looked formidable, the two little
orphans showed no signs of fear. As soon as they sat
down, the man asked them, "What brings you here?"
They replied that they had come for the jade to build a
jade igloo. "Oh, and what, may I ask, do you have to get
the jade with?"*

*"Well, we don't have anything to get the jade with, but
we came to get it anyway."*

*"Oh. How could you have come with nothing to get
the jade? What do you have anyway?"*

*"We don't have anything. We simply decided to come
for the jade and here we are."*

*"Oh, I see," the man sitting on the floor said. "As for
me, I will show you something. After I show you what I
have, I am sure you will show what you do have. You
must have something!"*

*"We don't have anything. We simply decided to come
for the jade and here we are."*

—Robert Nasruk Cleveland and Donald Foote,
Stories of the Black River People

A Place Called Red Dog

▲▲▲▲▲▲▲▲▲

Pretty spectacular, isn't it?" Duane Gingrich gestures across the valley toward the Wulik Peaks. Snow squalls drift off to the west, trailing a rift of turquoise sky. Caught in the sudden slant of October sun, the peaks blaze an incandescent white. Beyond, the DeLong Mountains, a fraction of the western Brooks Range, stretch to the horizon.

Looking over this arctic landscape, you can't help being struck by its pure, impersonal beauty—a beauty that asks nothing of the admirer, and offers nothing in return. This is a place without beginning or end, beyond mortal constructs.

"You can see the whole operation from here," says Gingrich, manager of the Red Dog mine construction project. The valley below, 100 miles north of the arctic circle, hundreds of miles from any road system, is a beehive of activity on this bright autumn day in 1989. Bright yellow bulldozers labor back and forth; huge-wheeled dump trucks come and go in steady, antlike procession; a crane swings girders into place on the growing skeleton of a multistoried building.

"That will be the workers' accommodations. Gym, swimming pool, library, the works," Gringrich points. "The mill will be going up there." In the fresh snow at my feet are the precise, catlike prints of a red fox. Ptarmigan trails also dot the slope, and the fox trail intersects them, tracing the story of this morning's hunt. There is no telltale scattering of feathers to mark a kill.

"And here"—Gringrich indicates a narrow side valley to our right, draining the hill we stand on, and a rather ordinary mountain beyond—"is Red Dog. You're standing on the second richest lead and zinc deposit in the world."

Off to the southwest, a thin dun-colored ribbon winds off across the tundra—the newly completed haul road leading fifty-odd miles to the mine's port site on the Chukchi Sea, the first cross-country road in the northwest arctic, an area the size of Indiana. A tractor trailer, tiny with distance, crawls uphill, the bulk of an incoming construction module on its back.

Bush pilot Bob Baker couldn't have guessed the magnitude of his find. Flying low over the DeLong Mountains one day in 1968, he noticed a reddish cast to the hills in a certain creek drainage. A part-time prospector himself, Baker figured the colors meant some sort of mineralization. He relayed his observation to Dr. Irving Tailleur of the U.S. Geological Survey, and when Tailleur eventually filed a public report on the deposit, he dubbed it Red Dog in honor of O'Malley, Baker's reddish mongrel. Baker never saw the report; shortly after his discovery, he was killed flying a mercy mission.

Red Dog remained little more than a name on a map until September 1975, when the U.S. Bureau of Mines issued a press release describing its preliminary findings there. Cominco American, a subsidiary of the Canadian mining giant, happened to have an exploration crew on the Seward Peninsula, less than 200 miles away. Although the actual Red Dog site was part of lands being considered for inclusion in the national park system, and so unavailable for staking, Cominco acted at once. Geologically promising land nearby was open to claims, and there was a fair chance that Red Dog would end up outside the park boundaries.

The geologists quickly recognized Red Dog was no ordinary ore body—was in fact a sedimentary deposit similar to their rich Sullivan mine in British Columbia, a top producer for eight decades. In 1976 Cominco began a systematic exploration of the DeLongs, a program that continues to this day.

Later in 1976, NANA, the newly formed Native corporation for the northwest arctic region, filed a land selection claim with the Bureau of Land Management, as provided for by the Alaska Native Claims Settlement Act—a claim that included Red Dog. Cominco, however, kept their interest active. In 1978, the federal government's hold on the Red Dog area expired, and Cominco American drove in their stakes, launching a court challenge of NANA's claim, which was, in their lawyers' opinion, less than airtight.

The ownership issue was settled by the passage of the Alaska National Interest Lands Conservation Act in December 1980. NANA came away the winner, but they needed a mining company to explore, evaluate, and develop their deposit. Cominco, with its experience in arctic mining and knowledge of the area, was the logical choice.

The corporations negotiated for two years, finally shaking hands in early 1982. Meanwhile, serious groundwork had continued— millions of dollars invested in feasibility studies, development and construction options, a mile-long aircraft runway near the mine site, a search for investors. Geologists probed the vast deposit, and over half the test holes produced "spectacular" results. Cominco and NANA seemed to be sitting, almost literally, on a gold mine.

But not everyone in the NANA region was convinced that a mine at Red Dog—or anywhere else in the northwest arctic, for that matter—was a good idea. Certainly there was the lure of jobs. The largest employer in this region was the school district, hardly a major industry. Seasonal work in commercial fishing and construction supplemented an economy based largely on federal and state assistance programs. Most of the northwest arctic's 5,000 Eskimos still depended on the land for food, clothing, shelter—and cultural identity. To many villagers, NANA's and Cominco's joint plan for development represented a threat to both their subsistence lifestyle and to local sovereignty. In Noatak, the community nearest the mine site (roughly thirty-five miles away) there was talk of withdrawing from NANA. Elders spoke out, and high school students (some of them mine) confronted visiting officials with pointed questions about environmental impact. Just three years later, I'd see many of them on my visit to the mine site, hard-hatted and smiling, talking about new boats and snowmobiles.

Questions about the environment were worth asking. Red Dog lay just outside the boundary of the Noatak National Preserve, one of the largest undisturbed watersheds in the world. Eskimo subsistence hunters had ranged across the entire area for centuries. Each spring and fall, thousands of migrating caribou passed over these hills; would the proposed road deflect them from their chosen path, as roads elsewhere had done? Then there was the problem of water contamination. The creeks around Red Dog were near the headwaters of the Wulik, one of Alaska's finest arctic char rivers, and the proposed haul road would have to cross scores of streams and fifty miles of fragile wet tundra, where bulldozer tracks would leave permanent scars. The selected port site was even more sensitive—within the Cape Krusenstern National Monument, one of the richest, most unique archeological sites in North America.

Cominco and NANA officials traveled village to village, assuring everyone that they would not have to choose between subsistence and development; the land would be protected regardless of cost—millions of dollars invested in environmental studies and safeguards—and shifts at the mine would even be arranged to allow for regular subsistence leaves to the workers' home villages. And, as the northwest arctic's people got used to the idea of Red Dog, opposition faded away.

There were other obstacles to be overcome before construction could begin. One was another challenge of ownership, this based on a boundary dispute with the neighboring North Slope Borough. The court ruling in favor of the newly established Northwest Arctic Borough (formed in anticipation of tax revenue from Red Dog) cemented NANA's claim.

Another problem was that Cominco needed major financial backing to get started—nearly half a billion dollars. The port road alone had been estimated at one million dollars for each of its fifty-two miles. When the project's backers, a consortium of international banks, came up with just $200 million, Red Dog's future seemed in doubt. Then Cominco persuaded the Alaska State Legislature, flush with oil revenues, to allocate $175 million to fund the transportation system—road, ore conveyor, and port.

Cominco and NANA were in business if the required permits (more than ninety) could be obtained. Most of these concerned environmental protection, and not all were mere formalities. Clearance to build the port would, in fact, eventually require an act of Congress to shift the boundaries of the Krusenstern National Monument.

The plans called for an open pit mine feeding a mill that would produce flourlike concentrates of zinc, lead, and silver. The concentrate would be trucked to the port and stockpiled, then barged out in the brief ice-free season—mid-June through October—to customers around the Pacific Rim. The mine's scheduled opening in 1990 would coincide with a predicted lapse in worldwide zinc production and a corresponding favorable market.

Although two decades had passed between discovery and development, once construction began in summer of 1987, the pace was dizzying. Between July and October, eleven bargeloads of equipment and supplies were landed at the port site. Over a hundred bulldozers, loaders, scrapers, and heavy trucks; three million gallons of diesel fuel; three million pounds of explosives for blasting, four million dollars in spare parts; a million dollars' worth of spare tires—numbers as huge as Red Dog itself. Ensearch Alaska Construction spearheaded the road project, surging forward at the rate of 100 feet *an hour*, twenty hours a day in the bright arctic summer nights. Conditions were difficult—unstable tundra overlying permafrost, with nearly 500 stream crossings—what amounted to icy swampland. To save time and expense crossing such terrain, the road was engineered as a single lane with regular turnouts. First, a layer of geotextile fabric (special cloth spooled on huge rolls) was laid down to keep the road from sinking; then a bed was built up with gravel quarried from pits along the route. Over two and a half million cubic yards of fill and two million square yards of geotextile were needed, along with six miles of steel culvert and nine major bridges.

Alaska Construction and Oil, an industry journal, proclaimed, in a cover story called "Doing Battle with the Arctic," that the Red Dog road project "can be compared to some of the amazing military construction projects accomplished during wartime." The story went on, "Imagine a general addressing his construction battalion: 'Your mission is to establish a beachhead and punch through fifty-two miles of gravel road. You must rip, drill, and blast every cubic yard of embankment material. You will work in summer, fighting hordes of mosquitoes. Then you will work in winter, fighting 30-degree-below-zero temperatures. Good luck, gentlemen.'"

Although they were racing the onset of winter and using machinery that could rip down a mountain, Ensearch was compelled to follow strict environmental standards. Nothing outside the road and gravel pit corridors was to be disturbed; the land on each side would remain as it had for eons—marked only by game trails, wide as the sky—

if forever redefined by the thin dusty ribbon running through its heart.

By Thanksgiving there was a drivable road connecting the port and mine site; Ensearch had come through sixty-nine days ahead of schedule. Now Green Construction, the main contractor for the mine project, could get to work. The first crews began in January's bitter cold and darkness. By spring of 1988 the operation was in full swing, with more than a dozen companies working long shifts in the growing warmth and light. The runway that had languished for five years now buzzed with activity; huge Hercules cargo planes and smaller aircraft ferried men and materials in a steady stream.

There were actually several main projects, all moving forward at breakneck speed. While heavy equipment crews stripped off overburden and prepared the actual deposit for development, others labored at a dam to contain the huge amount of waste water and runoff that the mine would create. Meanwhile, the living-quarters complex grew at a seemingly exponential rate, assembled from 300 prefabricated modules built far to the south.

The mill itself, which would be completed in 1990, was also modular; built on the West Coast, these seven units, as large as 1,600 tons and eight stories high, were barged north to the port site, then moved up the haul road on gigantic crawlers—specialized vehicles of the type used by NASA to transport launching platforms. Assembled, the plant will define the state of the art in both technology and efficiency. Meanwhile, at the port site, the concentrate storage building, the world's largest manmade structure north of the arctic circle, nears completion. Off to the side, dwarfed by comparison, stand two fuel tanks holding nearly half a million gallons.

If all went according to plan, Red Dog would be operational sometime in 1990. At full production, it will be the world's second largest supplier of zinc and lead, shipping 750,000 tons of ore concentrate annually. There will be steady jobs for over 300 workers, many of them from the NANA region; altogether, the mine should inject $5 billion into Alaska's economy over its fifty-year lifespan. In this time of declining oil revenues and statewide economic woes, Red Dog, many Alaskans say, is a bright spot on the horizon.

A bright spot. I try to see it that way. People need jobs, and just now there aren't nearly enough. One of the reasons so many young men and women languish around their home villages, playing basketball, riding snowmobiles in circles, and drinking is that there is so little opportunity. In this age of planes and computers, they can't live entirely off the land. Food stamps and welfare, even if they're part of the current subsistence cycle, do as much damage as good. In that sense, Red Dog could be a good thing.

But then I remember a week before this visit, looking down on the haul road for the first time. I was flying with Paul Weisner in his little Cessna, skimming over the Mulgrave Hills, boxed in by a low overcast. "There it is," Paul said. Visibility was bad on that gray day, and the stretch of tundra below us enormous; still, that narrow little slash of gravel seemed almost fluorescent, fading into the distance east and west below us. Paul banked toward the mine, and we said little as we looked down. I recognized a place I'd hunted caribou years before, and then the hill where I'd broken down once, and another where I'd seen a sow grizzly with three cubs. All three spots were within sight of the road. I looked over at Paul, muttering to himself under the engine's roar. He'd lived in the northwest arctic for twenty years, and he was a practical man—an engineer who'd done some mining himself. "God damn," he was whispering over and over. "God damn." It's just a road, I told myself. The country's still there. I turned my face to the window, and neither of us said anything more.

Lulled by the heated truck cab and the whir of wheels over gravel, I listen to Duane Gingrich speak pleasantly as we drive toward the port site. We've just had a fine meal at the mess hall, and a complete guided tour of the mine site. It's all been very impressive, the company's concern for the environment especially so. Here is work and a future for The People, part of the bridge they need. As we drive west toward the sea, the tundra stretches away on either side, its quiet patina of tans and whites luminescent in the arctic dusk, the hills beyond cast in deep blue shadow. A lone red fox pauses to watch us pass, then trots on his way. Distant caribou raise their heads, then return to their grazing.

And I think over again
My small adventures
When from a shore wind I drifted out
In my kayak
And thought I was in danger.
My fears,
Those small ones
That I thought so big,
For all the vital things
I had to get and to reach.

And yet there is only
One great thing,
The only thing:
To live to see in huts and on journeys
The great day that dawns
And the light that fills the world.

—Song from the Kitlinguharmiut
(Copper Eskimo), *The Report of the
Fifth Thule Expedition 1921-1924*

The Last Light Breaking

▲▲▲▲▲▲▲▲▲

I saw the sun today for the first time in two weeks. My students and I watched at the classroom window as it rose above the Waring Mountains. The ten of us stood facing south, feeling its orange glow on our faces, knowing that, in less than an hour, it would set again. *"Aarigaa,"* smiled one boy. "Longer days. Pretty soon springtime."

The winter solstice has just passed, and three months of deep cold remain; but in a sense, he's right. We're already gaining seven minutes of sunlight a day, and by the end of next month the afternoons will be long and bright, warming steadily, until the last darkness fades into the intoxicating, eternal light of arctic spring. Most people would call it winter; the land stays frozen white until mid-May. But then, magically, almost overnight, the snow collapses into grimy, shrinking heaps, and the Kobuk breaks free with a roar, great pans of ice drifting seaward, shattering steadily in the still, blue light. The sandhill cranes flap north in stiff-winged chevrons, their huge, rusty-doorhinge voices filling the sky with the promise of summer.

This June will be my fifteenth in the northwest arctic. The thought surprises me, even though I can account for the time; letters, notebooks, and photographs prove the passage of years, as do the broken sleds, the caribou horns piled outside my cabin. Still, I often feel like I fell asleep on a winter day and awoke to the cry of geese overhead. Fifteen years, one year, a thousand—the land remains the same. It's easy to forget that life is measured in heartbeats.

When I first saw Ambler in 1979, it was a different place. Two hundred and fifty people lived there then, a hundred fewer than today. Most of the buildings that stand now didn't exist back then—the freezer plant, the Kobuk River Lodge (once Erik's Ambler Trading), the city office, the fuel project, the clinic, the Traditional Council building, two small stores, the new Friends church, and more than twenty cookie-cutter modules that the Eskimos call "housings"—prefabricated dwellings with tile floors, paneling, and indoor plumbing, much superior to the sort that Nelson Greist and others received. (Those units were so shoddy that they were eventually given away.) The gravel runway up the hill, once lit by hand-placed kerosene flare pots, now boasts an automated electrical system, and there are high-tech navigational beacons to guide pilots in. The Alaska Department of Transportation laid a grid of gravel roads through town, complete with stop signs. Of all the changes that have come, those half-dozen red metal octagons bemuse me most; they stand scattered about the village, propped against a huge backdrop of sky and land, insisting on human order and limitation. I look at them and wonder if I should laugh or weep.

Erik VanVeenen sold Ambler Trading ten years ago and moved to Fairbanks, though he continued to guide in the Kobuk. Apparently his bullshit tax finally wasn't enough to keep him in the store business, though I don't know for sure. We lost touch with each other long ago. The last I heard, the wardens had seized his plane and suspended his big game guiding license for a handful of violations. He's gone from the Kobuk country, a dozen years after someone had told me, only half-joking, that Ambler would one day be renamed Erik, Alaska.

Nelson Greist's potato farm is slowly returning to the spruce forest it came from. After two years of trying, Nelson could never coax the ground to yield more than a few bushels of spuds, some smaller than the span of a silver dollar. The land simply refused to become something it wasn't. Control Data officials yanked their subsidy; Nelson shrugged and went back to commercial fishing. Now he uses the old farm as a fish camp, and sets his subsistence gillnet in the eddy nearby. The windblown summit of Ingichuk Mountain is still without a ski lift.

I've been back to Noatak village a few times over the years, coaching or refereeing basketball games, and the *Napaaqtugmiut* are as expansive and hospitable as ever. Some people still ask me when I'm coming home, though I've been gone for six years. Noatak's story of progress is much the same as Ambler's: more buildings, more people, more "housings." Many of the villagers work at the Red Dog mine, just thirty-five miles through the mountains to the north.

Red Dog, all $400 million worth, began production on schedule in 1990. Although the world zinc market hasn't been as strong as projected, several hundred people, many of them local Inupiat, have found work at the mine, jobs that pay anywhere from $20,000 to $50,000 a year. Dozens of new snowmobiles in Ambler and Noatak attest to the new affluence, but so do increased levels of alcohol and drug abuse. Family life is disrupted by the shift schedule, which takes one or even both parents away from home for weeks at a time. Some people grumble about unfair hiring practices.

Although both Cominco and NANA pledged scrupulous regard for the environment, heavy metal effluent from the mine did find its way into the Kivalina River last year, enough to tint parts of the normally transparent river a cloudy yellow, and scandalize Kivalina residents who depend on the river for drinking water and subsistence fishing. The federal EPA stepped in and shut down the mine until the problem was solved, but chances are more difficulties lie ahead. Some Noatak hunters complain that the caribou don't winter near the road corridor as they once did. There are whispers, too, about impending health problems among workers who sometimes can't avoid breathing the metal-rich powdered ore concentrate.

More to the point is the Red Dog haul road, officially known as the DeLong Mountain Regional Transportation System. The "System" is administered by the Alaska Industrial Development Export Authority and the Alaska Department of Transportation and Public Facilities. Pro-development forces see the Red Dog road as the first strand in a web that would eventually link other mineral claims (including, perhaps, the gargantuan coal deposits near Point Lay) to the coast.

Further on, the Department of Transportation hopes to connect Nome (on the Seward peninsula) to the pipeline haul road, which bisects Alaska 300 miles to the east. The state easement is still there, passing through the upper Kobuk just a few miles from Shungnak. Each year a bill to support the project is presented to the Alaska State Legislature in Juneau. So far, it's been voted down. I once heard a young DOT engineer say that pushing through that road would be, for him, "a dream come true." Many *Ivisaappaatmiut* also want a road, including my students, who say they want Ambler to grow. McDonald's on the Kobuk? Why not? Cars? Sure. Lower prices? *Aarigaa*. Even Minnie Gray nods and smiles when I ask her if she wants it, too.

The rich copper and jade deposits between Ambler and Shungnak are only part of the prize. Back in the hills are those thousands of mineral claims, and doubtless more undiscovered. Maniilaq, the elders say, saw it all coming: the growth of Ambler into a huge city, spurred by white strangers who seek something precious in the ground. When I ask Nelson if it's the jade or copper, he shakes his head. "They never find it yet," he says. "Anyone gonna find it. Maybe even you."

At the edge of sleep, images blur together: stop signs and wolves; rusting oil drums and silver light; the roar of snowmobiles; old women casting their nets in the dusk. *Anyone gonna find it.* But there is an emptiness beneath. Though it comes from the land, I can best explain in human terms. Years ago, I loved a woman; I watched her for days, all the while holding my breath, waiting for a sign, a gesture of any sort that showed she noticed me. The sign never came, though I kept watching long after she was gone.

And so I often find myself alone, far back in the country, waiting as a hopeful lover might—kneeling on the tundra of the Redstone one September evening, facing north into the wind as darkness fell; or riding down the Imelyak valley on a dazzling April morning, laughing like a fool, overwhelmed by the pure, cold radiance before me. I once sat below the curve of an arête playing my harmonica, imagining that the mountains bowed and whispered back. Even now, the sudden appearance of a grizzly becomes a talisman; I tell myself that a burst of winter light is a secret nod meant only for me.

Of course, I know better. The land offers itself equally to all things—caribou and wolf, flower and man; the emptiness comes from knowing that I'm no more important to what I love than any tree or stone. That's as it should be, but love is seldom rational.

Fourteen years ago, at the foot of Natmaktugiaq Pass, I held a ram's horn in my hands, set it down, and walked away. It must still be there, slowly wearing down in the wind and rain, disappearing from itself as it becomes part of everything. This is the only love the land offers: she refuses our embrace, and then, when we are past love, hope, and even knowing, takes us in her arms after all.

Epigraph Sources

△△△△△△△△△

Page 16: From *The Report of the Fifth Thule Expedition 1921-1924,* Copenhagen, Gyldendalske Boghandel, 1929.

Page 20: From the narrative of Lawrence Akisaqpak Gray, in *Lore of the Inupiat,* Mendenhall, Sampson, and Tennant, editors, Northwest Arctic School District, Kotzebue, pp. 3-4 and 9.

Page 32: From Robert Nasruk Cleveland's *Stories of the Black River People,* National Bilingual Materials Development Center, University of Alaska Anchorage, p. 57.

Page 40: From the autobiography of Edna Hunnicutt, *The Eskimo Storyteller,* by Edwin S. Hall, Jr., University of Tennessee Press, Knoxville, p. 63.

Page 52: From James Wells's *Ipani Eskimos,* Alaska Methodist University Press, Anchorage, 1974, p. 65.

Page 64: Clarence Wood, in conversation, May 25, 1992.

Page 82: From "Nathlook: Susie, My Name," in Lela Kiana Oman's *Eskimo Legends,* Alaska Methodist University Press, Anchorage, 1975, pp. 20-21.

Page 90: From the narrative of Oolyak (Stonewall Jackson), in Louis Giddings' *Kobuk River People,* Department of Anthropology and Geography, University of Alaska Fairbanks, 1961, pp. 59-60.

Page 100: From "Nathlook: Susie, My Name," in Lela Kiana Oman's *Eskimo Legends,* p. 28.

Page 108: From "Lights of the Caribou," in Lela Kiana Oman's *Eskimo Legends*, p. 85.

Page 114: From the autobiography of Edna Hunnicutt, *The Eskimo Storyteller*, p. 55.

Page 124: From Robert Nasruk Cleveland's *Stories of the Black River People*, p. 90.

Page 130: From the autobiography of Edna Hunnicutt, *The Eskimo Storyteller*, p. 70.

Page 140: From James Wells's *Ipani Eskimos*, p. 12.

Page 146: From the narratives of Joe Immaluuraq Sun and Lawrence Akisaqpak Gray, *Lore of the Inupiat*, Mendenhall, Sampson, and Tennant, editors, pp. 27 and 45.

Page 160: From "Nathlook: Susie, My Name," in Lela Kiana Oman's *Eskimo Legends*, pp. 28-29.

Page 164: From the autobiography of Edna Hunnicutt, *The Eskimo Storyteller*, pp. 59-60.

Page 172: From the autobiography of Edna Hunnicutt, *The Eskimo Storyteller*, pp. 70-71.

Page 176: From the autobiography of Edna Hunnicutt, *The Eskimo Storyteller*, p. 65.

Page 188: From the autobiography of Edna Hunnicutt, *The Eskimo Storyteller*, pp. 60-61.

Page 196: From James Wells's *Ipani Eskimos*, p. 72.

Page 200: From Robert Nasruk Cleveland's *Stories of the Black River People*, pp. 165-66.

Page 208: From *The Report of the Fifth Thule Expedition 1921-1924*.

SUGGESTED READING

Anderson, Douglas, Wanni Anderson, Ray Bane, Richard Nelson, and Nita Sheldon. *Kuuvangmiit Subsistence, Traditional Eskimo Life in the Latter Twentieth Century.* Washington, D.C.: National Park Service, 1977.

Berger, Thomas R. *Village Journey: The Report of the Alaska Native Review Commission.* New York: Hill and Wang, 1985.

Blackman, Margaret B. *Sadie Brower Neakok, an Inupiaq Woman.* Seattle: University of Washington Press, 1989.

Carey, Richard Adams. *Raven's Children: An Alaskan Culture at Twilight.* New York: Houghton Mifflin, 1992.

Cleveland, Robert Nasruk, and Donald Foote. *Stories of the Black River People.* Anchorage: National Bilingual Materials Development Center, University of Alaska Anchorage, 1980.

Giddings, J. L. . *Kobuk River People.* Fairbanks: University of Alaska Press, 1961.

———. *Ancient Men of the Arctic.* New York: Alfred A. Knopf, 1967.

Gray, Minnie Aliitchak, Tupou Pulu, Angeline Newlin, and Ruth Ramoth-Sampson. *Old Beliefs (Taimaknjaqtat): Upper Kobuk.* Anchorage: National Bilingual Materials Development Center, University of Alaska Anchorage, 1980.

Hall, Edwin S., Jr. *The Eskimo Storyteller: Folktales from Noatak, Alaska.* Knoxville: University of Tennessee Press, 1975.

Henning, Robert, Lael Morgan, Barbara Olds, and Penny Rennick, eds. *The Kotzebue Basin.* Anchorage: The Alaska Geographic Society, 1981.

Kotzebue, Otto von. *Voyage of Discovery in the South and Behring [sic] Straits, for the Purpose of Exploring a Northeast Passage, in 1815-1818.* Weimar and London, 1821.

Lee, Linda, Ruth Ramoth-Sampson, and Edward Tennant, eds. *Qayaq, the Magical Traveler.* Kotzebue: Northwest Arctic Borough School District, 1991.

Lopez, Barry. *Arctic Dreams: Imagination and Desire in a Northern Landscape.* New York: Charles Scribner's Sons, 1986.

Mendenhall, Hannah, Ruth Ramoth-Sampson, and Edward Tennant, eds. *Lore of the Inupiat: The Elders Speak.* Kotzebue: Northwest Arctic Borough School District, 1989.

Oman, Lela Kiana. *Eskimo Legends.* Anchorage: Alaska Methodist University Press, 1975.

Oswalt, Wendell H. *Alaskan Eskimos.* San Francisco.: Chandler and Sharp, 1967.

———. *Eskimos and Explorers.* Novato, Calif.: Chandler and Sharp, 1979.

Ramoth-Sampson, Ruth, and Angeline Newlin, eds. *Maniilaq.* Anchorage: National Bilingual Materials Development Center, University of Alaska, 1981.

Rasmussen, Knud. *The Report of the fifth Thule Expedition 1921-24. The Danish Expedition to Arctic North America.* 12 vols. Copenhagen: Glydendalske Boghandel, 1929.

Roberts, Arthur O. *Tomorrow is Growing Old: Stories of the Quakers in Alaska.* Newberg, Ore.: The Barclay Press, 1978.

Wells, James K. *Ipani Eskimos: A Cycle of Life in Nature.* Anchorage: Alaska Methodist University Press, 1974.

ABOUT THE AUTHOR

▲▲▲▲▲▲▲▲▲

Nick Jans is a teacher and writer in Ambler, Alaska, an Inupiaṭ Eskimo village on the edge of the western Brooks Range. In the past fourteen years, he's also managed a trading post, worked for a big-game guide, and traveled over forty thousand wilderness miles. *The Last Light Breaking* is his first book.

The son of a career diplomat, Jans grew up in Europe, Asia, and Washington, D.C. In 1977 he graduated from Colby College in Maine. In 1979 he visited Alaska in

Author Nick Jans with arctic char in the Brooks Range

Photo by Steve Pliz

search of adventure and found a home instead. He took a year off from the bush in 1986 to study creative writing at the University of Washington.

Jans's nonfiction and poetry have appeared in *Alaska* magazine, *National Fisherman, Christian Science Monitor,* and *Rolling Stone.* His work has won several awards, including the 1987 James Hall Prize for fiction from the University of Washington. Recently he was named a contributing editor to *Alaska* magazine.